Madeleine was a true bridge builder; and if ever we've needed some, now is the time.

Philip Yancey, author, *Vanishing Grace: Bringing Good News to a Deeply Divided World*

Many thanks to Sarah for capturing the beauty and complexity of Madeleine L'Engle who influenced millions of readers around the world to always light candles in the darkness.

Catherine Hand, film producer, *A Wrinkle in Time*

Science and religion. Faith and fiction. The gift of both/and is the Madeleine L'Engle legacy I, and many a Christian creative, has benefitted from most, and Sarah Arthur's *A Light So Lovely* takes a deep dive into the fullest meaning of L'Engle's beautifully complex perspective, displayed in all of her work, but most famously in *A Wrinkle in Time*. Through Arthur's insight, we see that L'Engle's thinking makes room for the kind of wonder readers will want to hold on to.

Why do we humans insist on codifying who and what God is, and who He is in us? In *A Light So Lovely*, Arthur explores the ways in which Madeleine L'Engle repeatedly pushed against this tendency and, in doing so, created stories that revealed a God without limits, one who we could trust implicitly at any age, and share openly without apology.

Nikki Grimes, *New York Times* YA and children's bestselling author

I've waited a long time for a book about Madeleine L'Engle's spiritual legacy and *A Light So Lovely* was entirely worth the wait. In this book, Sarah Arthur explores L'Engle's wide and generous spirituality with her bestselling books, her lectures, her public work, but wisely also with her relationships and her devoted readers' (myself among them!) remembrances, all while placing her within the larger narrative of her time and place. *A Light So Lovely* beautifully and honestly illuminates one of the most important and creative writers of our time.

A compelling portrait of an author whose commitment to challenging our labels and categories, to bridging the imagined divide between sacred and secular, is as relevant today as ever.

Sara Zarr, YA author

What fun, and what a delight it is to gain these fresh and careful insights into the life of Madeleine L'Engle, literary icon and dear friend whose imagination and storytelling has become the stuff of legend! Through the narratives of the friends and family who knew and loved her, Sarah Arthur has used her vivid gifts of words and insights to bring Madeleine to life. Read, enjoy, and be enlarged by these stories.

Luci Shaw, author, *Thumbprint in the Clay*

This book has a secret. It's a magic word—one so small you might overlook it. The word? *And.* It's everywhere in this book, marking how Madeleine L'Engle reconciled what we have divided. Like L'Engle's vision, Arthur's book is for believers *and* unbelievers. Readers *and* writers. Fans of science fiction *and* romance. People of faith and people of science—and those who love both of those languages. Girls, boys, women, men—those in their forties *and* twenties, *and* who are also still five, capable of wide-eyed, childlike faith. This intimate introduction is so full of wisdom, it will rejuvenate newcomers to L'Engle's work *and* her most faithful fans. I'm grateful for Arthur's homage to a personal hero: It's a joy to read *and* a reminder to live with wild imagination.

Jeffrey Overstreet, author, *Auralia's Colors* and *Through a Screen Darkly*

An eminently readable, deeply lyrical, and thoroughly necessary examination of a literary luminary in the context of her faith. Arthur helps illuminate not just L'Engle's own writings but the wider promise of the Anglican tradition.

Tara Isabella Burton

In *A Light So Lovely,* Sarah Arthur gives us the heart of Madeline L'Engle's legacy, that the Christian life (like Christ's life) is subversive and beautiful, and that hope is sometimes deceptively ordinary. We need this reminder now more than ever.

Brian Bantum, Associate Professor of Theology, Seattle Pacific University

A
LIGHT
SO
LOVELY

Also by Sarah Arthur

*Between Midnight and Dawn: A Literary Guide to
Prayer for Lent, Holy Week, and Eastertide*

*The Year of Small Things: Radical Faith for
the Rest of Us* (with Erin F. Wasinger)

*Light Upon Light: A Literary Guide to Prayer
for Advent, Christmas, and Epiphany*

*At the Still Point: A Literary Guide
to Prayer in Ordinary Time*

Mommy Time: 90 Devotions for New Moms

*The God-Hungry Imagination: The Art of
Storytelling for Post-Modern Youth Ministry*

*The One Year Coffee with God:
365 Devotions to Perk Up Your Day*

*Walking Through the Wardrobe: A Devotional Quest
into* The Lion, the Witch and the Wardrobe

*Dating Mr. Darcy: The Smart Girl's
Guide to Sensible Romance*

*Walking with Bilbo: A Devotional
Adventure through* The Hobbit

*Walking with Frodo: A Devotional Journey
through* The Lord of the Rings

A
LIGHT
SO
LOVELY

THE SPIRITUAL LEGACY OF
MADELEINE
L'ENGLE,

Author of *A Wrinkle in Time*

SARAH
ARTHUR

ZONDERVAN

A Light So Lovely
Copyright © 2018 by Sarah Arthur

Requests for information should be addressed to:
Zondervan, *3900 Sparks Dr. SE, Grand Rapids, Michigan 49546*

ISBN 978-0-310-35340-9 (softcover)

ISBN 978-0-310-35343-0 (audio)

ISBN 978-0-310-35342-3 (ebook)

Cover design: Jeff Miller | Faceout Studio
Cover photo: madeleinelengle.com
Interior design: Kait Lamphere

First printing June 2018 / Printed in the United States of America

For my young sons,
Micah and Sam.
May you tesser well.

I have never yet fully served a book.
But it is my present joy to try.

Madeleine L'Engle

CONTENTS

FOREWORD

by Charlotte Jones Voiklis

The first time I spoke with Sarah, I cried. While it doesn't take a great deal for me to have tears break the surface these days, as Sarah asked me questions and shared her thoughts about my grandmother, I knew I'd met someone with deep compassion, curiosity, and intellect. We talked about my grandmother's life: her habits, milestones, and challenges, and what we each knew to be her impact on others. As we spoke, what moved me to tears was Sarah's willingness to look at Madeleine and accept her as a full and flawed human being; an icon and iconoclast, not an idol.

In *Walking on Water: Reflections on Faith and Art* (a 1980 book that, as Sarah demonstrates, shook a generation of evangelical Christians with its expansive view of God's love for all of creation), Madeleine warns that "paradox is a trap for the lazy," and she challenges her readers to embrace "both/and." Sarah takes on the challenge and structures her book as a series of what are commonly thought of as binary choices: sacred/secular, faith/science, fact/fiction, and more.

A Light So Lovely explores what Madeleine L'Engle has

meant to a generation or more of Christians who are searching for something that would restore their faith and who found that something in Madeleine's language of wonder, hope, and joy, often to a rather extraordinary degree. The book combines interviews with artists and friends (and I'm sure I'm not the only one who cried during a conversation with Sarah), close readings and analyses of not just Madeleine's works but of the changing Christian landscape of the past fifty years, and Sarah's own memoir-like interventions and reflections that illustrate how the universal is grasped only in the particular.

The book not only (and beautifully) serves as a guide to Madeleine L'Engle's spiritual legacy for Christians, it also (and intriguingly) can serve as a guide to evangelical Christian culture for the uninitiated. Although Madeleine's religious upbringing and most of her practice was mainline, she found in a variety of religious communities, including evangelical circles, an audience of interlocutors that challenged and enriched her own theological understanding. For the reader whose only exposure to evangelical thought is the most recent flurry of news and analyses, looking at the conversations—sometimes friendly, sometimes vitriolic—that Madeleine and evangelicals engaged in over decades, and the ways in which her writing helped so many of the "wavering, wounded, and wondering," is illuminating. Sarah looks at the "heresy" of universalism, the debates over science and religion, and the ways in which Madeleine's themes of art and joy were received. Sarah's discussion makes the stakes involved in those issues more legible, and I have a deeper understanding of and hope for the excavation of additional common ground.

Sarah likens the broad body of Madeleine's work to a pod of whales, swimming together, communicating with each other, with the occasional one breaching the surface of the ocean. I love the metaphor, and believe it to be true. The cluster of messages that all of Madeleine's books transmit include: you are loved, you matter, your questions are important, your joy fulfills a promise, fear not. This is indeed good news.

INTRODUCTION

We draw people to Christ not by loudly discrediting what they believe, by telling them how wrong they are and how right we are, but by showing them a light that is so lovely that they want with all their hearts to know the source of it.

Walking on Water

Though I've always been a reader, it was my Wheaton College roommate, Chloe, who introduced me in a serious way to the works of Madeleine L'Engle. This was the early '90s; Madeleine's bestselling novel, *A Wrinkle in Time*, was already thirty years old; and while I'd heard of it as a teenager, I'd assumed it was purely science fiction, which wasn't my genre. (I'm also pretty sure I'd read her 1965 novel, *The Moon by Night*, in junior high—I can still visualize the '80s teen-romance edition—but I didn't connect it with the author of *Wrinkle* at the time.) From Chloe I now learned that young-adult fiction wasn't all L'Engle had written. I began to devour some of L'Engle's nonfiction, including *The Rock That Is Higher: Story as Truth*, as well as her landmark book on faith and art, *Walking on Water*. And I quickly realized here was an iconoclast: a Christian who spoke openly about Jesus yet was also a Newbery Medal winner, no less.

I can't overstate the gift Madeleine was to this mainline evangelical. I was raised in small towns by a Presbyterian minister-father and a mother who was a public-school math teacher. Sometime in my elementary years my parents experienced a charismatic renewal that supercharged our faith. It made us curiously bilingual: we were mainliners, but we could speak "evangelical." My engagement with more conservative strands of Christianity came through Christian concerts and camps and bookstores and radio stations; I wanted to *be* Amy Grant. But every day at 5:00 p.m., my parents would turn on National Public Radio's *All Things Considered*, and that too was part of our Christian engagement with the world.

Then I arrived at Wheaton, where I encountered a small but vocal subset of students who insisted that the "things of the world" and "the things of God" were divided into strict binary categories. And God only worked through the latter. Thus, we could only believe this *or* that: only creation *or* evolution, only faith *or* science, only fact *or* fiction, only sacred *or* secular, only conservative *or* liberal, only Scripture *or* nothing, only, only, only. For the first time in my life I was being told—continually, fervently, bluntly—what God *can't* do.

I was baffled. Was this the *evangel*, the good news?

Enter Madeleine. Here was a Christian author who could function quite unperturbedly from inside paradox, who dared to question the assumption that all things must be either/or. Why can't it be both/and? What is this nonsense about "secular"? Why can't God use those things if God wants to? Why can't

God speak through this or that person (if God can speak through a donkey, for instance)? Who says?

"Our faith is a faith of vulnerability and hope," she wrote in *A Stone for a Pillow*, one of her Genesis commentaries, "not a faith of suspicion and hate. When we are looking for other people to be wrong in order that we may prove ourselves right, then we are closing ourselves off from whatever unexpected surprises Christ may be ready to offer us. If we are willing to live by Scripture, we must be willing to live by paradox and contradiction and surprise."[1] I had found a Christian author who spoke my language of wonder, who somehow didn't see things such as scientific discovery or artistic expression as threats to the gospel but rather windows by which we can see God's light from new and exciting angles. Through her relentless, generous, prolific art and her obvious love for Christ, Madeleine managed to challenge the narrow, reactionary, oddly unjoyful posture of some believers to the extraordinary world God made—and to the extraordinary God who made it.

My English professors, I'm thankful to note, had a L'Engle-esque way of engaging paradox too. It was clear they had tremendous respect for her—indeed, to this day many of her papers are housed in the special collections of Wheaton's Buswell Memorial Library. She was still a force, still writing. She made visits to campus, where at one point she signed several books for me. And the more I learned about her, the more I realized, like so many hundreds of thousands of readers, that I had found an icon. Not an idol whom one worships—as Madeleine herself would correct us—but a window, a person whose life and faith points beyond itself to Christ.

My first adult decade was spent in full-time youth ministry, during which I regularly wondered if I could better influence the next generation by writing middle-grade fiction myself rather than collecting parental permission slips for paintball. While reading Madeleine's Crosswicks Journals—*A Circle of Quiet, Two-Part Invention,* and so on—I continued to feel an affinity with a writer who shared a love for the Anglican-Episcopal liturgy, for living in community, and who insisted on story as a vehicle for truth.

Eventually I shifted to a writing career and a seminary degree, regularly circling back to Madeleine's *Walking on Water,* in which she called the act of writing a form of prayer. "To be an artist means to approach the light, and that means to let go our control, to allow our whole selves to be placed with absolute faith in that which is greater than we are"[2]—a description that named my experience of the creative process *exactly.* Even today, when I read in *A Circle of Quiet* about how tired she was as a mother of small children (like me) trying to balance a writing career (like me), I cry. At times it's hard to tell where her influence leaves off and my own thinking begins.

● ● ● ●

And I'm not alone. Time and again, as I traverse ever-widening, overlapping circles of writers and culture-makers, Madeleine's name comes up as an author who changed the course of someone's journey. In fact, as this project got underway, I began asking people, "Can you point to a moment when Madeleine L'Engle influenced your vocation as an artist? Or saved your stumbling faith? Even saved your life?" And the stories have come pouring in, stories of how Madeleine helped a new generation reclaim the light of Christ in an increasingly murky and polarized faith. Thus, central to each chapter of this project are interviews with such people as writer Sarah Bessey (*Jesus Feminist*), artist Makoto Fujimura (*Culture Care*), YA novelist Sara Zarr (*Story of a Girl*), children's and YA author Nikki Grimes (*Bronx Masquerade*), and film critic and novelist Jeffrey Overstreet (*Auralia's Colors*)—and that's just a sampling.

Her spiritual legacy is not limited to my own generation, however. Madeleine herself was part of a group, formed in the '80s, known as the Chrysostom Society, a fellowship of Christian writers that gathered regularly to encourage one another in an often challenging publishing industry. Its membership has changed over the years, but among them have been such literary voices as Philip Yancey, Luci Shaw, Eugene Peterson, Stephen Lawhead, Richard Foster, and Emilie Griffin. Back in 2004, while Madeleine was still alive, I approached some of them at the biannual Festival of Faith and Writing at Calvin College about contributing to a collection of remembrances in her honor. I pictured her like a great ship at night under the stars, lit from bow to stern, passing over the horizon; we needed to point and say, "Watch! Don't miss her! There she goes!" But the timing wasn't right; I wasn't certain I could find a home for such a book. And so I let it drop, the moment passed, the ship slipped away and, on a September day in 2007, she was gone. She was eighty-eight years old.

A dozen years later, it's been fascinating to circle back to some of those same writers and ask, "Who was the Madeleine you knew? What's your favorite story about her? What were her quirks, her blind spots? What was her signature contribution to the way Christians talk about faith, story, art, and science today?" Remembrances by Philip Yancey and Luci Shaw, in particular—as well as Madeleine's longtime housemate Barbara Braver (not a Chrysostom Society member, but a fine poet in her own right)—have seasoned this project with more than mere personal insights. They've helped us take the long view, to not settle for merely riding along with the contemporary pendulum swings of public vitriol. They encourage us to face our cultural moment the way Madeleine would have: resolutely, lovingly, with an ear for how God is calling us to engage the darkness *in spite of* our weaknesses—or even, like *A Wrinkle in Time*'s Meg Murry, *because* of them.

Here's the ultimate paradox: God uses imperfect people, in every generation, at each unique point in history, to accomplish his purposes. "My grace is sufficient for you," God told the apostle Paul in 2 Corinthians 12:9, "for my power is made perfect in weakness." As the rhetoric on social media, in politics, and in social discourse increasingly polarizes us from one another, we aren't allowed to have weaknesses: only power, only the correct ideas, only a bluster and bravado devoid of repentance. And yet that's not how God chooses to act in the world. Born a helpless infant to poor Middle Eastern refugees, God in Christ took on our limitations; power became vulnerability; holiness touched the dirt and stench and darkness of humankind with relentless love. In the words of one of Madeleine's favorite Bible verses, "The light shineth in darkness; and the darkness comprehended it not" (John 1:5 KJV).

I now understand that Madeleine's embrace of paradox was something unique and new—not just to me, but for an entire generation. For Madeleine, if paradox is at the heart of the gospel—what she called "the technical impossibility" that "Jesus of Nazareth was wholly man as well as wholly God"[3]— then we shouldn't be surprised that paradox is precisely where God meets us in the rest of life too. She taught us that God can be at work in the sacred *and* secular, truth *and* story, fact *and* fiction, faith *and* science, religion *and* art—and we must not foreclose on how Christ will choose to work, nor through whom. The disciples were nothing if not surprised by this very thing ("Nazareth! Can anything good come from there?" Nathanael asked the disciple Philip in John 1:46). And why, Madeleine would ask us, should we be any different?

It's astounding how a deep dive into the pantheon of her works only shows just how often, and consistently, the above themes echo throughout her life and writing. Each work is like a whale singing its whale song to the others, all together a kind of pod swimming in more or less the same pattern on the same trajectory.[4] Every so often a whale breaches and earns public attention—most notably, of course, *A Wrinkle in Time*—but below the surface (and Madeleine loved to speak of what's submerged in our subconscious, that massive iceberg), the work is among its thematic peers. One amongst a larger body. Part of a consistent whole.

●　　●　　●　　●

My chief task in writing this book not only has been to understand her way of thinking about the intersection of things like story and truth, art and religion, and so on, but also to locate her within a larger narrative. How did she shape the way people of faith today engage and discuss those things? If it weren't for

Madeleine, how would those conversations be different? What were her most lasting contributions?

To that end, I've found it helpful to trace her journey through seven key movements, which provide the shape and structure of this book:

Chapter One—We'll survey her life and works as a whole, attempting to identify her spheres of influence, both as a cherished friend and mentor as well as a complex, flawed human being.

Chapter Two—We'll dive into her story where many readers do, with *A Wrinkle in Time*—a book that, like Madeleine herself, somehow bridges the often vastly different worlds of sacred and secular in American culture.

Chapter Three—We'll step back and trace her own spiritual formation as a child through the influence of great stories that gave her hints and glimpses of God's truth.

Chapter Four—We'll track the life-changing impact of scientists on her conversion to Christianity when she was a youngish write-at-home mom.

Chapter Five—We'll chart her profound spiritual influence on others during her prolific middle age, particularly her continued assertion that artistic practice is a religious vocation.

Chapter Six—We'll make the difficult turn toward her personal challenges later in life—the loss of her son, among other things—and her troubling propensity to blur fact and fiction.

Chapter Seven—Finally, we'll identify the ways that Madeleine attempted to battle the darkness, especially in her own soul, and to cling with resolute desperation to the light.

Through all of these movements I'll continually circle back to the people who knew her, as well as to a new generation influenced by her journey. And I'll ask the question: What does her story mean for us, now, in our own unique moment?

• • • •

Even when we take the ten-thousand-foot view, it's hard to map the scope of Madeleine's tremendous spiritual legacy, one that we're only just now, roughly ten years after her death, beginning to grasp. My young sons are growing up in a time when cultural lines are being marked in the sand with both virtual and actual bullets (and yet, is our time any different than other episodes in human history?). Thus, I want my sons to develop L'Engle's ability to embrace paradox, which allowed her to think and believe and say things that both fundamentalists and non-Christians alike insist are impossibilities. I want them to learn how to push their fellow Christians, in particular, to stop telling the world what God can't do.

Her most quotable statement is still urgently true: "We draw people to Christ not by loudly discrediting what they believe, by telling them how wrong they are and how right we are, but by showing them a light that is so lovely that they want with all their hearts to know the source of it."[5] For a new generation that has known nothing but the highly contentious political and religious climate of contemporary American culture, embracing Jesus in paradox is nothing short of good news.

And that's the crux of this book. Madeleine was no stranger to the stresses and battles we find ourselves fighting every day, as Christians, as artists, as thinkers, as human beings. Indeed, she often claimed, "The idea of God is not easy at all. I mean, I have to hang on till my nails are bloody to keep believing in God . . . If I believe in God wholly and completely for two minutes every seven or eight weeks, I'm doing well."[6] This is an astounding statement. How do you put one foot in front of the other, much less produce a phenomenal corpus of literature, when the road seems so dark? How do you continue to affirm the presence and goodness of God? Those are the questions animating these pages.

So let's strike a match, light a candle. Let's illuminate the life and legacy of this extraordinary woman such that we experience both the grace and the struggle that helped her shape a generation and beyond. Because ultimately it's not her own light we're drawn to, but the light of Christ she lifted up, however imperfectly, to the world. By knowing her better, we might better understand our own particular darknesses, in this unique chapter of American history, and how we're called to be light-bearers too.

Chapter One

ICON *and* ICONOCLAST

All of us who need icons—and I am convinced that
all artists do—also need an iconoclast nearby.

A Circle of Quiet

Sitting on my desk is a signed copy of *The Rock That Is Higher* from one of L'Engle's Wheaton College visits. That semester our chapel seating assignments were by first name. Not only was I smack in the middle of maybe seven rows of Sarahs, but also every girl in my balcony row was Sarah Elizabeth (apparently, our conservative parents thought they were being unique in a generation of hippies that named children "River"). For fun we would lean over the balcony and call "Hey, Dave!" and watch several dozen guys in one section all turn and look. All those biblical names . . . we were drowning in unremarkableness.

Into that mix came Madeleine L'Engle, a giantess in a great flapping dress of patchwork colors; I couldn't even properly pronounce her name. If she spoke in chapel or gave a lecture in an English class, I don't remember it. What I do remember is a tall woman sitting at a table in the bookstore blinking her large eyes like a wise and vigilant owl. She insisted on inscribing the book with my whole name, first and last, because, as one of her characters says in *A Wind in the Door*, "if your name isn't known, then it's a very lonely feeling."[1] Names and naming are of theological significance, Madeleine asserted: it's "one of the impulses behind all art; to give a name to the cosmos we see despite all the chaos."[2] Naming is how we are known and seen in the world, not only by people, but by the God who knows us and makes us unique from one another.

She signed a copy of her 1992 novel *Certain Women* for my mother as well—again, using my mother's first and last name. There is nothing rushed about the handwriting. It's careful, painstaking, elegant. There may have been a hundred people behind me in line, there may be a thousand stories of Madeleine encounters just like mine, but in that moment, one young woman and her mother mattered.

●　　●　　●　　●

If we are to understand Madeleine's spiritual legacy, not merely her biography, we must begin with a brief sketch of her life.

Madeleine L'Engle Camp, named for various forbears, was an only child, born in New York City on November 29, 1918, at the end of the Great War. Her father, Charles Wadsworth Camp, was a war veteran and theater reviewer who also wrote potboiler mysteries; her mother, Madeleine Hall Barnett, a pianist. Her parents had been married for at least a decade by the time she came along, "and although I was a very much wanted baby," Madeleine L'Engle wrote, "the pattern of their lives was already well established and a child was not part of that pattern."[3] It was, she often said, a lonely childhood.

Her parents attended plays and operas in the evenings and thus slept in late and dined late—without Madeleine. "I remember my parents coming, night after night, to kiss me good night and goodbye in their evening clothes, Father often with his top hat, looking like a duke, I thought."[4] The only exception to these separate worlds was Sundays, when the family attended Episcopal worship services and dined together. While Madeleine knew she was loved, she became, by sheer circumstances, a solitary child whose closest human companions were a devoted Irish-Catholic housekeeper, Mary O'Connell (whom the family called "Mrs. O"), and books.

Remember this. When you picture the confident celebrity who insisted on inscribing people's full names—hundreds of names, all over the country, decade after decade—remember the small child eating supper alone in her room, reading.

Her memoirs, such as *A Circle of Quiet*, tell how she bounced from school to school throughout childhood, including a miserable few years at an English-run Anglican boarding school in Switzerland, where her parents dropped her off without warning. Chapel services were required and decidedly boring—the only lasting benefit, she later claimed, being her daily exposure to the glorious language of the Anglican Book of Common Prayer, "badly read by one of the mistresses." Thankfully, her teachers "couldn't quite ruin the language of the great poets of the sixteenth and seventeenth centuries."[5]

While a student, she wrote and illustrated stories, as a coping strategy, when she should've been doing schoolwork—an author in the making. As her granddaughters, Charlotte Jones Voiklis and Léna Roy, describe in *Becoming Madeleine: A Biography of the Author of* A Wrinkle in Time *by Her Granddaughters*, Madeleine's childhood journals emphasize her astonishing drive not merely to write for fun but to make a *career* of it. Inspired by Emily in L. M. Montgomery's *Emily of New Moon* (one of her all-time favorite books), she wrote in her journal at age fifteen, "I, Madeleine L'Engle Camp, do solemnly vow this day that I will climb the alpine path and write my name on the scroll of fame."[6]

It wasn't until high school at Ashley Hall, back in the States, that she finally flourished among genuine friends and caring teachers, ultimately attending Smith College from 1937 to 1941. There she embarked on more earnest literary studies under the tutelage of such scholar-authors as Mary Ellen Chase. It was from Chase that Madeleine grasped "that anybody who was seriously considering writing as a profession must be completely familiar with the King James translation of the Bible, because the power of this great translation is the rock on which the English language stands."[7]

Madeleine's father died in 1936, when she was just seventeen, of pneumonia complicated by gas-damaged lungs from WWI. Finding no comfort or community in the Episcopal churches she visited during that time, she eschewed organized religion and became, for lack of a better description, a deeply unhappy, deeply moral, artist-agnostic—who also happened to read the Bible because her writing professor at an otherwise irreligious college told her to.

After college she seriously pursued a career in theater, which paid just enough for her to start writing novels on the side. She credited those earlier boarding-school days with the ability to write amidst communal chaos: "The result of this early lesson in concentration is that I can write anywhere, and I wrote my first novel on tour with a play, writing on trains, in dressing rooms, and in hotel bedrooms shared with three other girls."[8] In 1944 she met a tall, striking young actor named Hugh Franklin while touring with a production of Anton Chekhov's *The Cherry Orchard* (he later became famous playing Dr. Charles Tyler on the television soap opera *All My Children*). Hugh was kind and unassuming and clearly liked her; and after various fits and starts, they married in 1946. Together they continued to live in New York City.

Madeleine now dove into writing exclusively; her first novels—*A Small Rain* and *Ilsa*—came out in 1945 and 1946. By that point she had dismissed both her maiden name (Camp) and her married name (Franklin) as pen names, opting instead for "Madeleine L'Engle." When she was with Hugh, however, they were known as the Franklins.

Not long after they were married, the couple bought a farmhouse "of charming confusion" (as Madeleine often described it) that they named Crosswicks, in Goshen, Connecticut. They moved there full time in 1951 for nearly a decade, running the local general store and raising their young children: Josephine, Bion (named for Madeleine's maternal grandfather), and their adoptive daughter, Maria, who joined the family in 1956. Madeleine often pointed to those years as her most difficult season: attempting to parent small kids, run a business, and maintain a writing career while receiving numerous rejections, all of which put more irons in the fire than she could attend with grace.

She also found herself questing for spiritual answers, eventually making small but significant steps toward Christian faith and practice—a story we'll explore in more depth as this book progresses. Suffice it to say, her spiritual journey cannot be teased out from her vocational trajectory as a writer, and neither were more uncertain than during that decade. When, on her fortieth birthday, she received yet another publishing rejection, she says, "I covered the typewriter in a great gesture of renunciation." But then, she realized, her "subconscious mind was busy working out a novel about failure." So she uncovered the typewriter again. "In my journal I recorded this moment of decision, for that's what it was. I had to write. I had no choice in the matter. It was not up to me to say I would stop, because I could not."[9] She was meant—nay, *called* by a power beyond herself—to be a writer. "It's easy to say you're a writer when things are going well. When the decision is made in the abyss, then it is quite clear that it is not one's own decision at all."[10]

Her season of publishing rejections ended with her sudden celebrity status upon being awarded the 1963 Newbery for *Wrinkle*. The family returned to New York City while keeping Crosswicks as a summer home. Madeleine was back in a Manhattan apartment once again; but instead of reading books alone in her room, or scribbling them on the side, she now wrote them for an audience of millions.

● ● ● ●

From that point on, Madeleine's career was marked by prodigious output: upwards of sixty titles, everything from middle-grade, young-adult (YA), and grown-up fiction, to poetry, memoir, and creative biblical commentary—including the occasional children's picture book. And that doesn't include her unpublished journals or letters, her numerous forewords, afterwords, or contributing essays. Nor does it include her many public addresses, several of which have been anthologized. (At one point while researching this project, I narrowed down my Madeleine-related interlibrary loan options to forty-seven. From *seven hundred*.) A quick survey of her works follows here, to help us get our bearings:

Before the publication of *Wrinkle* she had a half dozen novels under her belt, scattered throughout the 1940s and 1950s, including the first in the Austin Family Chronicles (*Meet the Austins*, 1960). But once *Wrinkle* hit the shelves in 1962, she wrote whatever she wanted, roughly a title per year and in no particular order—an astonishing feat, considering the pressures of the publishing world to deliver more of the same winning series. In fact, *A Wind in the Door*, which directly follows the events of *Wrinkle*, didn't appear for another eleven years, in 1973, with subsequent titles appearing even later: *A Swiftly Tilting Planet* in 1978, *Many Waters* in 1986, and *An Acceptable Time* in 1989. Together they are sometimes known as the Time Quintet.

Novels featuring the Murrys (the original family of *Wrinkle*) and O'Keefes (descendants of Meg Murry and Calvin O'Keefe) became known as her "Kairos" line, or stories that blur the normal bounds of time and space. The Austin tales (of which *The Moon by Night*, 1964, was the first book she published after *Wrinkle*; and of which *A Ring of Endless Light* earned a Newbery Honor in 1981) were dubbed her "Chronos" line:

that is, stories taking place in real time, in our world, with only hints of science fiction or magical realism. Sometimes she connected the Kairos and Chronos storylines through ancillary characters—yet another example of Madeleine refusing to be forced into either/or.

Keep in mind, that's just her fiction for children and teens. Novels for adults, like *Certain Women* (1992) and *A Live Coal in the Sea* (1996), were fewer after her success as a children's author, yet still significant.

Meanwhile, Madeleine began publishing creative nonfiction with *A Circle of Quiet*, the first of her memoir-esque Crosswicks Journals, in 1972—and suddenly she found another niche. Now her audience included not just the young adults she originally wrote for, but also their grown-up selves as they attempted to make sense of their religious beliefs and vocations on the ground, in their everyday lives. *The Summer of the Great-Grandmother* followed in 1974 (about the decline and death of her mother) and *The Irrational Season* (1977), about the liturgical year; all of which culminated with *Two-Part Invention* in 1988, the story of her forty-year marriage to Hugh and his death of cancer in 1986.

Sprinkled throughout these releases were books like *Walking on Water*, *The Rock That Is Higher*, and her midrash-style commentaries on Genesis (*And It Was Good*, *A Stone for a Pillow*, and *Sold into Egypt*). To be honest, I have no idea how her publishers kept up.

All told, Madeleine's corpus has sold in the tens of millions—and continues selling.

●　●　●　●

We must not forget: this is the same woman who claimed to have been "an unsuccessful, nonachieving child at school, unappreciated and unloved by teachers and peers alike."[11] What she missed out on in a lonely childhood she more than made up for in her middle and later years as a successful author who traveled the world.

After Hugh's death, she continued to teach dozens of writing workshops, creating a fellowship of ardent student-disciples. To many of them she opened her home and, in some cases, her life, hosting various reunion dinners and other gatherings at her Manhattan apartment, surrounded by a menagerie of cats and dogs.

Madeleine in person was, by all accounts, larger than life. Tall, with an astounding self-confidence and stage presence, despite her claims to be physically clumsy, she had a straightforward, almost oracle-like way of speaking. *Publisher's Weekly* writer Jana Riess (*Flunking Sainthood*), in her interview for this book, described having dinner with Madeleine when the author gave the 1991 commencement address at Wellesley College: "She was outspoken, and I think that kind of took a person by surprise. She had a lot of opinions about everything from *Jesus Christ Superstar* to movies that were currently playing." Philip Yancey laughed when I asked him to describe his initial impressions: "When she wasn't around, some of us in the Chrysostom Society sometimes called her Dame Madeleine, because she had that imposing presence. She fulfilled that stereotype. She had strong opinions, she tended to make pronouncements. She was intimidating at first meeting and then gradually over the years as I got to know her I realized there's a soft person and a very welcoming person underneath."

Her students described her as "fierce in her faith," a woman who physically projected a "sense of wonder."[12] Poet Luci Shaw, L'Engle's lifelong friend, wrote:

> What the world saw was a powerful woman, large-hearted, fearless, quixotic, profoundly imaginative, unwilling to settle for mediocrity. Tall and queenly, she physically embodied her mental and spiritual attributes. Some of us remember occasions when, in church during Advent, at her home church, All Angels' in Manhattan, she rose to full height, spread her arms wide like the Angel at the Annunciation, and declared, "Fear not!" in a tone that allowed no gainsaying.[13]

Meanwhile, "Madeleine got more done in one day than most people accomplish in four," writes one of her goddaughters, filmmaker Cornelia Duryée Moore; "I watched her write the entire first draft of [*Certain Women*] in two weeks."[14] One of her writing students says, "Her five-foot ten-inch frame possessed twice my energy, endurance and creative stamina"—adding, "One day I found her in bed, somewhat tired; she had been a little ill, but still managed to dictate some seventy letters that day."[15] A day or evening spent with Madeleine at Crosswicks or her New York apartment ended with Compline, that simple ritual of communal Scriptures and prayer from the Book of Common Prayer.

Who on earth has *nineteen* godchildren? Madeleine did—among them many adults that she sponsored in their Episcopalian catechism. Hearing their stories, one gets the impression that half the aspiring artists on the Upper West Side, most Protestant poets, and a good portion of evangelical college students around the country converted to Anglicanism or some form of liturgical something before she was done with them. She also attended more weddings—couples that she, herself, introduced to each other—than seems humanly possible.

Madeleine also cultivated an ability to travel just about anywhere. As a young girl, when she wasn't off to boarding school or traveling in Europe with her parents, she spent a great deal of time near Jacksonville, Florida, surrounded by her mother's extended family and history. In adulthood she seemed at ease (or at least at a truce) with country life at Crosswicks, though she preferred the city. Travels to Europe, South America, China, and elsewhere marked her later years, before health issues slowed her down. She found something to talk about with most everyone, able to converse equally well in art, theater, and music as well as science, theology, and philosophy. She could hold her own as a commencement speaker at her "secular" alma mater, Smith College; but she was also at home in a place like Wheaton—despite the fact that conservative fundamentalists, as we'll discuss in the next chapter, became some of the most acidly vocal proponents of banning her books.

On her best days, she was openhearted and generous to people of all ages. Paul Willis of Westmont College remembers hosting Madeleine at his home during one of her college visits: "Before dinner she held a Q&A session with all of the neighborhood children, in which she sat in a big stuffed chair and they all sat on the floor." L'Engle scholar Carole Chase describes Madeleine keynoting a family retreat in the mountains of North Carolina, where the children flocked to her on the way to dinner: Madeleine carefully addressed each child individually before moving on. Jana Riess, recalling the Wellesley College visit, depicts a celebrity who turned down dinner with the college president because she had already agreed to dine with Jana and her friends.

Remembrances of Madeleine by friends, colleagues, and students approach hagiography. She was a "transformational light," a "bright shining star," a grandmother, mentor, minister, spiritual director, trusted advisor, Wise Woman, and guide, "maybe more than a little like the angelic presences in *A Wrinkle in Time*, Mrs Who, Mrs Whatsit, and Mrs Which, who had ways of bringing out the best in their earthly students by magnifying the students' inherently good qualities."[16]

If she's beginning to sound like an idol, that's because, for many, she was.

●　　●　　●　　●

But this was not the sum total of Madeleine. One of my favorite questions for those who knew her is "What were her quirks, her blind spots?" Paul Willis, speaking to me of her Westmont College visit, describes how "she passionately spoke twice in chapel on the text 'Judge not,' but when I had lunch with her she went on and on, just as passionately, about how she couldn't stand the current president of [another evangelical college] and was not going to give another dime to that school."

Paul also showed her Westmont's C. S. Lewis wardrobe, which had been owned by the great author of the Chronicles of Narnia himself. Incidentally, another Lewis wardrobe stands on prominent display at the Marion E. Wade Center at Wheaton College—although, purportedly, Lewis's personal secretary, Walter Hooper, claimed that Westmont's was the real inspiration behind the wardrobe in *The Lion, the Witch and the Wardrobe*.[17] "She got a real kick out of that," Paul recalled, "being fully acquainted with Wheaton College's pride in their own wardrobe. I can still see her standing in front of the wardrobe and chuckling and chuckling. I think it appealed to a delightfully wicked part of her."

Her temperament was certainly a force to be reckoned with. In a rare instance of honest critique, one writing student admits, parenthetically, "She could be dismissive and scathing when appalled or hurt."[18] Madeleine herself admitted to being moody. She could also be blunt. Her decisiveness was not always leveraged graciously. Luci Shaw describes sharing a newly written poem with her one afternoon—a moment of vulnerability for any writer. After a brief pause, Madeleine said, without preamble, "Take off the last three lines."[19]

Then there's the infamous *New Yorker* profile by Cynthia Zarin in 2004, three years before Madeleine's death. It was less than flattering, in which Madeleine's children reportedly hated *Two-Part Invention* for being unrecognizable. In which they likewise claimed to detest the Austin Family Chronicles for hitting too close to home while painting an overly idealized portrait of their otherwise tumultuous domestic life, in which her son Bion is said to have died from the effects of an alcoholism that Madeleine never acknowledged. Later, children's books biographer Leonard Marcus's 2012 collection of interviews, *Listening for Madeleine*, only served to bolster Zarin's earlier assessment, with reflections from Madeleine's children and grandchildren in particular that paint a much more complex portrait of the beloved author.

It's a hard pill to swallow, as we'll discuss further in chapter six. Needless to say, her students and ardent fans, and even many of her colleagues, with whom she worked closely, found those interviews distressing. The *New Yorker* profile was not, they insisted, the Madeleine they knew. And yet one could argue that the people with the real chops to speak are the ones who were closest to her, her family, who loved her in spite of their painful history. Who was the real Madeleine? Or could she be, like paradox itself, both/and?

I've come to realize that in all of these different incarnations, Madeleine was not merely code switching. All of these things were who she was. As her granddaughter Charlotte Jones Voiklis says, "She had such a fluid mind that she didn't have to prioritize by saying, I'm this first and these other things are secondary. She was always a 'both/and' thinker, not an 'either/or' thinker."[20] Madeleine was both icon and iconoclast; which is another way of saying she was, like the rest of us, utterly human.

If I learned anything in divinity school, it's that the uncomfortable places, the troubling questions about faith and Scripture and life and humanity, are exactly where we need to drill down. Focus there, where it bothers you. Dig where it disturbs you, and see what God is doing. Because if God isn't at work in the hard places—*in spite of* God's own people, not just *because of* them—then why bother with any of it?

For Madeleine, if God speaks anywhere, God speaks everywhere, even through things, places, and people we least expect—including those with whom we vehemently disagree, including the idols and icons that at times disappoint us by being just as imperfectly human as we are.

• • • •

If we need icons, we also, Madeleine insisted, "need an icon-oclast close by"[21]—someone who takes our precious little idols—those ideas we think we understand, those cherished convictions—and smashes them. It was her own husband, Hugh, she claimed, who played this role for her, often critiqu-ing her first drafts so incisively that she stormed off in a rage. But there were others, friends and colleagues, whose way of seeing the world were not like hers. For Madeleine, one of those friends was Luci Shaw.

I've known Luci myself for well over a decade, ever since I first picked up her poetry collection *Polishing the Petoskey Stone* when I lived in Petoskey, Michigan, and then all but stalked her at the 2004 Festival of Faith and Writing at Calvin College. In the picture I took of us that year, she's smiling sheepishly while I suppress whoops of excitement: "I'm a rabid fan! I can't believe I get to meet you in person!" Then later, as I was curating the literary guides to prayer for Paraclete Press, we corresponded regularly: "Can I reprint this poem? How about that one? And that one?" When it came to my Christmas collection, *Light Upon Light*, I dubbed her the Patron Saint of Advent. She, meanwhile, endured all this graciously, the epit-ome of poetic generosity.

When I was approached about writing this book, there was absolutely no question: I had to set up an interview with Luci. She responded to my query immediately: "I'd love to talk to you about Madeleine, in all her complexity!" Finding the time was another thing: not only was there a three-hour time difference between Michigan and the state of Washington, but at almost eighty-nine, Luci is impressively busy, maintaining a rigorous publishing and speaking schedule that reminds me of, well, Madeleine. But finally we connected.

As Luci tells it, she and Madeleine met in the '70s at Wheaton College, where Madeleine was invited by the English faculty to speak at a conference on the arts. Luci was also a presenter. "Wheaton invited her to come," Luci explained, "and it was a bit of a risk. Because at that point it was—and Wheaton still is—very conservative; and some of her ideas sort of wandered beyond the usual boundaries of faith and belief. She had a wildly imaginative mind and sometimes that took her into territory that Wheaton might have considered dangerous."

Meanwhile, the only Wheaton College Madeleine had ever heard of was in Massachusetts. When the letter detailing her visit arrived, she discovered that this particular Wheaton was in the Midwest—and a premier Christian college, no less. "Someone explained to me that Wheaton was Evangelical. 'What's that?' I asked."[22] (Pause while the rest of us attempt to comprehend a time when someone in the United States could reach their fifties without ever hearing the word *evangelical*.) In typical Madeleine fashion, she went anyway—rather like a tourist on safari, or so I picture her—and to her own surprise, she found a new spiritual home. As Madeleine later told the Wheaton class of 1977 in her commencement address (she had just spoken at Smith College the day before), "Although Smith is my *alma mater* and I love it, I was not as at home there as I am with you. Nor could I say the same words there that I can say to you today. Because here at Wheaton, I'm able to be openly a Christian among Christians."[23]

It was at Wheaton, she claimed, that she learned a more

spontaneous way of praying beyond merely reciting the pre-scripted language of the Book of Common Prayer. And it was at Wheaton that she met Luci. They hit it off immediately. "We both loved the color green," Luci told me, chuckling. "We both loved baroque music, we both loved Bach, we both would play the Bach fugues." These may sound like trifles, but to Madeleine—raised among New York's musicians and litera-ti—it must have signaled someone with a shared culture. And, needless to say, they were both writers. Luci and her husband Harold had just started a new literary publishing company, Harold Shaw Publishers.

"We were hoping to focus on literary biographies, poetry, literary criticism, that sort of thing," Luci explained to me about those early years, "'literature for thoughtful Christians.' Madeleine told me that she'd written two books of poetry, and they both went out of print (I don't know why). I said, we would love to publish those books, and if you've got more recent poems that aren't in those books, we'd love to add those to the number of poems that have gone out of print. She was delighted. So we did that. It was our first project with her. It was called *The Weather of the Heart*." Luci would go on to work with Madeleine, as her editor and sometimes coauthor, on at least eleven books, including one about their decades-long friendship called *Friends for the Journey*.

But it was during one July visit to Wheaton, in 1977, that the two authors became very close. "Her granddaughter Léna was involved in a bad car accident," Luci told me, "and her life was in danger. Madeleine and I went for a long walk in a park and sat down and prayed together for Léna. She recovered. When we were able to pray together over something so pressing and so life-and-death, that cemented us." Roughly a decade later, both of their husbands died of cancer in the same year. "We did a lot of talking over the phone and catching up and understanding what we were going through," Luci recalled. "That brought us very close together."

This didn't stop them from disagreements, however, particularly over theology. Luci had been raised in an extremely conservative Christian home and church; needless to say, Madeleine had not. "One of the great things about my relationship with Madeleine," Luci said, "was that we sparred a lot around ideas and truths. We never quarreled, but we had long discussions in which she would take one position and I would take the other; and we nearly always ended up in the middle." Luci tells of editing sessions in which she would exclaim, "Madeleine, you can't say that to evangelicals!" But then, after Madeleine had explained and defended herself, Luci would conclude, "You *must* say that, exactly that way."

"Sometimes when we were involved in editing something and we had a strong disagreement, we'd come to the point when we understood each other, and then we'd stand up and sing the Doxology, almost spontaneously," Luci told me. I picture them seated at a paper-strewn dining table in Madeleine's New York apartment, late afternoon sun flooding the room, surrounded by cats and empty tea cups. And then suddenly these two literary giants—well, one an almost-giant in a flowing dress and the other a petite Brit with twinkling eyes—rise and belt out a hymn.

Luci captured it well when she wrote to Madeleine, in *Friends for the Journey*, "And you, on your part, can make radical theological statements with which I may disagree, but again, because of our bond of love we accept each other for who we are, flawed and failing, but always truth-seeking."[24]

Do you feel it, the quiver of longing? I'm guessing I'm not the only one who knows firsthand just how rare, how valuable, such a grace-filled, truth-seeking kind of friend is. Not an idol, not a mentor or spiritual director: a *friend*.

What would it look like to have friendships with those who are not like us, wherein we learn to argue well and lovingly—and yet at the end of the day we can still be friends? This is a lost art in our culture, particularly as we create ever narrower, taller, insular silos on social media, cut off from opposing viewpoints. With a mere click of a button we can "unfriend" and "unfollow" those with whom we disagree, and meanwhile we learn to studiously avoid those difficult topics at Thanksgiving dinner that could disrupt the false unity a sentimental holiday too often cultivates. False unity is no healthier than silos of like-mindedness.

We need iconoclasts, mentors, and friends that push us, that challenge our narrowness and yet still affirm our humanity. What would it mean to meet in person, on purpose, in good faith, with someone whose perspective is vastly different than ours? To argue face-to-face without rancor, without demeaning the humanity of the other? What would it mean to allow yourself to acknowledge areas where you might, in fact, *agree*? Or even more, to allow yourself at times to be persuaded—if not wholly to the other person's perspective—at least to meet halfway? This is what it means to live life with those who don't insist that everything, including our own persons, be either/or. Rather, we can be both/and.

This is the rare gift that Luci and Madeleine gave to each other. And we, in turn, are the beneficiaries.

● ● ● ●

In our digitized age, the word *icon* has become synonymous with a simple, universally recognized symbol, a kind of modern hieroglyphic shorthand. It's intended to reduce complexity and accelerate communication, especially when shared language or even literacy cannot be assumed. (For instance, long before they could read English, my sons, ages five and seven—both digital natives—recognized the Play icon, or button, on a tablet and knew its use.) But for Eastern Orthodox Christians throughout the centuries, the original meaning of *icon* is a painting that depicts a biblical character, story, or saint from Christian history—not merely as a symbol or shorthand, and certainly not as an object to be revered (again: that would be an idol), but rather as a window to a bigger reality.

For example, the vanishing point of a Byzantine-style icon is the reverse of the linear, Western European style of painting: it comes out, toward the viewer, rather than in, toward the painting's horizon. Psychology professor and author Richard Beck of Abilene Christian University describes it this way:

> As we stare into the icon the world we are looking into isn't shrinking or vanishing. Rather, it is *expanding* and *growing.* I like to call this *The Wardrobe Effect*, borrowed from the scene in C. S. Lewis' *The Lion, the Witch and the Wardrobe*, where the children move into and through a small space (the Wardrobe) to emerge into this vast expansive space (Narnia). An icon is trying to create, via reverse perspective, this same effect upon us. Heaven is more real and larger than this world.[25]

While he acknowledges that the early icon artists likely didn't know their perspective was the reverse of some other style, the implications are profoundly theological. Yes, one could argue that religious icons have a utilitarian purpose, to give the illiterate access to communication—in this case, access to God's Word in visual form; but they also provide literate believers with new ways of seeing, of comprehending, of meditating on the Word.

To many readers, Madeleine's works often have the same effect, as we'll discuss further in the next chapter. However, Madeleine would've resisted the metaphor of an icon applied to herself—especially since, in her words, "it is precisely because an icon touches on reality that it far too often becomes an idol."[26] And certainly she was idolized and adored more than she liked. Her longtime friend and housemate, Barbara Braver, talked with me about how Madeleine handled her own fame:

"Sometimes when you idolize somebody you don't really know them and you don't really want to because it would tarnish your idol. She did not take her celebrity as a measure of herself. She had clarity about who she was with her various gifts and weaknesses and failings and strengths, so she didn't need to look to everybody who idolized her in order to get some self-regard . . . Madeleine had compassion for people and interest in their particularity. She was not from a mold; she was very much herself, very much a character. She was interested in how other people were formed and made. Also, she had suffered some in relationships in her growing-up years . . . being left unexpectedly at a boarding school in Switzerland by her parents—that's a tough thing to have happen. She was very compassionate for people."

As both Luci and Barbara reiterated, "Madeleine would say, 'I'm grateful to be loved and appreciated. I don't want to be adored.'" For all her imperfections, there was something about her pithy way of communicating, about the unforgettable images, characters, and scenes she created, about her dogged insistence on pointing her readers and students to God's love, that tore down the idol others had made of her and turned it into an icon.

An icon is not a mirror, merely reflecting our own selves back to us. It's a window that points to light and truth *beyond* itself. It's not to be mistaken for the light. "He must become greater," said John the Baptist at the coming of Jesus into public ministry; "I must become less."[27] Beyond Madeleine was the bigger reality of God's presence in the world, God's particular love for each one of us. That's the light she wanted us to see.

We also must—like iconoclasts, like Madeleine herself—insist that what we had thought was inviolable (our cherished platitudes, our well-crafted doctrines) are, in fact, limited by our very humanity. "For now we see only a reflection as in a mirror," wrote Saint Paul in 1 Corinthians 13:12, "then we shall see face to face."

If Madeleine taught us nothing else, as both icon and iconoclast, it's that we are flawed and imperfect beings. It's not our own light we bring to any situation, but the light of Christ we attempt to shine on others.

The question becomes, what happens when the light makes others feel uncomfortable?

Chapter Two

SACRED *and* SECULAR

There is nothing so secular that it cannot be sacred, and that is one of the deepest messages of the Incarnation.

Walking on Water

One freakishly hot day in late September, I stop by my local Michigan library. I've put about forty-seven L'Engle-related titles on hold through interlibrary loan, which feels like the literary equivalent of ten Christmases; and I plop them all down at the desk like someone cashing in at a casino. The young man behind the counter grins and starts scanning.

"It's Banned Book Week. What's your favorite banned book?" he asks brightly, as if censorship is the juiciest gossip around.

I pause, flummoxed that he hasn't noticed all the L'Engle books he's so helpfully checking out for me. "Um, *A Wrinkle in Time* by Madeleine L'Engle?" I wave at the pile.

He perks up. "Cool!"

Ah, he recognizes the patron saint of banned books—and of librarians, for that matter. More importantly, he recognizes the name of an author who also happened to be unashamedly Christian. Who loved Christ. Who talked about Christ—in her life, in her books. And who won a Newbery anyway.

●　●　●　●

Over the years, *A Wrinkle in Time* has met with a dizzying array of responses: everything from publishers' rejections to high acclaim to vociferous censorship. When Madeleine was first trying to find a publisher, the story got rejected twenty-seven times (or was it thirty-two? Thirty-six? Her numbers changed every time she told the story) before it was picked up and published by Farrar, Straus and Giroux in 1962. In the years following she often described the various reasons why it had been turned down: it was hard to classify, it dealt with difficult topics like the problem of evil, and on and on. When I told my marketing-savvy husband, "Did you know that her original title was *Mrs Whatsit, Mrs Who, and Mrs Which*?" he said, without hesitation, "Well, that's why it got rejected, right there."[1]

Her book has been hard to categorize ever since. Leonard Marcus, in *Listening for Madeleine*, refers to *Wrinkle*'s "aggressively unorthodox mongrelization" of genres.[2] Is this for children? adults? Is it science fiction? fantasy? magical realism? religious? Whatever it is, like Madeleine herself, it doesn't stay within the strict categories we place on everything, those stringent binaries of either this *or* that. At times her writing makes us uncomfortable, forces us to question our cherished assumptions. Indeed, it's rather like the description of Aslan the lion in C. S. Lewis's Narnia Chronicles: good but not "safe."

Perhaps that's why, in both sacred and secular circles, Madeleine and her works have been suspect.

From the nonreligious side, people treated *Wrinkle* (and its author) as questionable because it was so obviously Christian— and not just vaguely "spiritual" either; but clearly, unequivocally Christian. When, for example, the main characters want to know who those "fighters" are that have squared off with the Powers of Darkness, one of their mentors, Mrs Who, quotes directly from the gospel of John: "And the light shineth in darkness; and the darkness comprehended it not" (1:5 KJV). "Jesus!" exclaims the youngest child, Charles Wallace. "Why of course, Jesus!" When editor Beatrice Creighton of Lothrop, Lee & Shepard was asked why she didn't publish *Wrinkle*, another editor remembered Bea saying something like, "Madeleine writes wonderfully well, but I just couldn't go along with all the religion business. I thought it got in the way of the story."[3]

Madeleine's own explanation was more poignant: "In the world of literature, Christianity is no longer respectable. When I am referred to in an article or a review as a 'practicing Christian' it is seldom meant as a compliment, at least not in the secular press. It is perfectly all right, according to literary critics, to be Jewish or Buddhist or Sufi or a pre-Christian druid. It is not all right to be a Christian. And if we ask why, the answer is a sad one: Christians have given Christianity a bad name."[4] Thus, the editorial gatekeepers, at publishing house after publishing house, practiced their own form of censorship in advance: they wouldn't even publish it.

It was Hal Vursell at Farrar, Straus and Giroux who took a personal liking to it, despite thinking it was "distinctly odd."[5] He gave it to an outside reader, who told him it was the worst book that person had ever read; but he nonetheless decided to give it a chance. No one was more surprised than Madeleine's own publisher when it won the 1963 Newbery.

Years later, children's author Lois Lowry said in a 2012 panel celebrating *Wrinkle*'s fiftieth anniversary, "Rereading the book quite recently I was startled because I had forgotten the religious references in it, the number of Christian references . . . And I'm not sure that that would be published today. Or that an editor might ask you to tone that down a bit. Or that the Newbery committee would say, 'It's not politically correct to give an award to a book that's so *Christian.*'" The panel's moderator, then New York Public librarian Betsy Bird—who herself had served on a Newbery Committee—agreed: "I don't think they would choose it. And it's for the very reasons that you said. And it's a pity, because it's a grand book. My respect for the committee that did select it just goes up all the more."[6]

After Madeleine won and catapulted from obscurity to literary wunderkind, she would tell how she was invited to various literary-artsy galas, and publishers would say, "Why didn't you submit *A Wrinkle in Time* to me?" And she'd respond, "Oh, but I did." And when they protested, she'd say, "I can show you the rejection letter."

But from the other side, the conservative Christian censorship was just as pronounced and much more public. How crushed she was that it was her fellow believers who loudly insisted on banning *Wrinkle* from libraries, schools, and churches. Their reasons were vast and largely uninformed. Parents complained, for instance, that high schoolers were secretly passing the book around for the "sex scenes." (Which, it turns out, were the scenes when Meg and her companions tessered, or traveled, to other planets. The teens assumed innuendo when Madeleine intended none, and the parents took their word for it.)[7] The book also contained witches, according to Madeleine's critics. "If you read the book," Madeleine said in a 1989 interview with religion journalist Terry Mattingly, "there is no way that they [Mrs Whatsit, Mrs Who, and Mrs Which] are witches. They are guardian angels—the book says so. You don't have to clarify what is already clear."[8]

Other detractors studied all her works extensively, bent on identifying what they felt was demonic and making a career out of "exposing" her. According to her critics—whom she dubbed "fundalits," short for "fundamentalist literalists"— Madeleine's fiction and nonfiction alike supposedly featured "communication with the dead, mind control, psychic healings, communicating telepathically with dolphins (a New Age favorite), goddess worship, witchcraft/shamanism, occult meditation, astral projection, divination, and more."[9] One of them concluded, "L'Engle's novels are not just pure fiction; they are spiritual poison for children, precisely because they are considered 'Christian.'"[10]

Madeleine said in a 2001 interview with the *New York Times*, "First I felt horror, then anger, and finally I said, 'Ah, the hell with it.' It's great publicity, really."[11] And yet, it's safe to wonder if she ever really reached the "finally" of that statement. For her, the conflict was a theological problem, a serious error on the part of her fellow Christians. "There is a new and troublesome fear of the imagination—though without it, how can anyone believe in the Incarnation, the Power that created all of the galaxies willingly limiting itself to be one of us for love of us! And this fear is expressing itself in a new kind of book burning and witch-hunting."[12]

Undeterred, Madeleine's critics virulently insisted that public libraries and schools, not just churches, should regard her works as evil. Madeleine found these attempts at censorship deeply disturbing: "If I believe that I am qualified to decide what the entire population of the United States, particularly Christians, ought *not* to be reading, am I not making an idol of my own judgment?"[13]

Idols again. How persistent our perennial inability, whether we inhabit religious or irreligious circles, to engage an author on her own terms. How reticent we are to allow her to be an icon—admittedly an imperfect one—through which God's light shines, rather than an idol to either worship or shun.

●　●　●　●

Recently I interviewed YA author Sara Zarr (*Story of a Girl*) about Madeleine L'Engle's influence on YA lit in general and on her own writing in particular. I was intrigued by Sara's reflections on the word "secular" in her preface to the new edition of Madeleine's *Walking on Water*, in which she tells of growing up in the '80s in Christian circles that were influenced by the rising evangelical subculture. "Strangely," she writes, "as much as I heard the word *secular* as a label on things that should be avoided by good Christians [such as pop music, prime time TV], I don't ever remember hearing the word *sacred*, its opposite. Instead, I heard the words *clean* and *safe* to describe what was not deemed worldly."[14] Like Sara, I'm struck by how wildly inadequate—and ultimately insupportable—that binary is. What book of the Bible qualifies, for one thing? (I'm reminded of the student whose unchurched mother discovered the copy of the Bible he'd been reading for youth group; she opened it randomly to the book of Judges and then forbid him to ever read the Bible again.)

"When I first decided 'I want to try and become a novelist,'" Sara told me, "I never really remotely entertained the idea that I would be a 'Christian' novelist. Because the books that made me want to write and gave me an emotional response—that felt like they were connecting to something real—were always just regular books." For Sara, those were "mainstream writers like Madeleine L'Engle, like Robert Cormier, even Judy Blume, Norma Fox Mazer, people like that who were writing YA realism. And as you may recall, in the '70s and '80s most YA was realism."

Sara remembers in the '80s there would be outcries over books that included things like sex; and authors fought against "the expectation that the book should have a purpose other than to tell the story of the book." Now, she sees the same thing happening, except in the other direction: "It's a time of a kind of secular Puritanism where having the correct thoughts and opinions is—and I may just be spending too much time in social media—but it seems like there's not a lot of room to be in the middle on things. It's like, 'You're for us or against us' on almost any issue."

For groups that have previously been marginalized, she recognizes this as a helpful corrective to voices that have been silenced in the past. But many younger writers "don't know we fought this battle before—as far as what gatekeepers thought was appropriate for teen readers—and consider it a triumph that now you can literally write about anything in YA." In particular, Sara said, "Christian writers, or writers of faith, should be free to explore the realities of the experience of being alive, on the full spectrum."

It's a rough guess, but the word *sacred*—meaning "holy," or "set apart"—may sound just a little too Catholic for many Protestants. It may evoke too much of the inaccessible nature of the Catholic God, whose face we cannot see without intermediaries, whose presence we sinners approach with fear and awe— rather than the kind, forgiving, nondenominational "Divine Butler and Cosmic Therapist" who knows us personally and forgives us anyway.[15] We don't want a God whose holiness renders him Other, in whose presence we feel unclean and unsafe. So we substitute other words for *sacred*; and then leverage an antonym, *secular*, that is likewise thin and unsupportable.

As spoken-word poet Amena Brown says, non-Christians don't get what Christians mean when they say *secular*. If Christians were to describe it, non-Christians would say, "Oh, you mean regular things."[16] As if God doesn't deal in regular things.

I reached out to children's and YA author Nikki Grimes (*Bronx Masquerade, Jazmin's Notebook, Dark Sons*) about how she navigates the artificial divide between *sacred* and *secular*. Nikki responded, "The answer is, of course, in the question. The phrase *artificial divide* is key, as Madeleine L'Engle understood better than anyone. The divide is, in fact, artificial, and one can simply choose to ignore it." She went on to explain: "Of course, early in my career, I worried incessantly about crossing some invisible line between secular and sacred in my work. But what I've realized, over time, is that as long as the presence of God is organic within a literary work, secular publishers are not bothered by it, nor do readers find that presence intrusive in any way." Questions Nikki asks herself include, "Is faith in God, and all that goes along with it, authentic to the character in your story? Are God-related occurrences organic within the framework of that story? Those are the only questions I need ask, and if the answer to both questions is yes, then the work can easily straddle secular and sacred publishing worlds."

Madeleine herself didn't make a distinction between sacred and secular—or at least, she didn't define them the way other people did. Madeleine's understanding of *sacred* encompassed every aspect of God at work in the world. "To be truly Christian means to see Christ everywhere, to know him as all in all."[17] There is no sphere where God is not, and thus no place where God is incapable of transforming what evil has deformed. And meanwhile God's beauty and truth and goodness speak through the most ordinary things, through their essential nature or "sheer quiddity," as C. S. Lewis called it. Madeleine wrote,

> Life cannot be separated into secular and sacred, that if God created everything, and called it good, then all of life is good, and only we can see it as sacrilegious. There is nothing which is, of itself, sacrilegious. Just as the act of making love can be sacramental, so can all aspects of our lives, even the most lowly. If we cannot pray in the bathroom, it is not likely that we will be able to pray anywhere.[18]

Philip Yancey reflected with me on how unique her perspective was compared to his own upbringing: "The church I grew up in was very much 'this world is not my home, I'm just a passin' through,'" he told me, "and as soon as you get saved it's all over: the rest of life is just gritting your teeth and managing to survive until that glory day when you cross into Beulah Land, wherever that is. And later I found that actually, no: God created this world, God loves this world, God wants us to thrive in this world. And that includes culture, beauty, and art." When it comes to Madeleine's unique legacy, he said, "I think Madeleine negotiated that divide very well because she was uncompromising about her faith and yet she was fully invested in thriving in this world and helping others to thrive."

● ● ● ●

As controversial Christian authors go, she was in good company. C. S. Lewis too was among those banned by fundamentalists and treated cautiously by the literati. At one point, someone sent her a clipping from a daily newspaper featuring a list of ten books that libraries should not carry because the books were somehow "pornographic." "On the list was one of C. S. Lewis's Narnia books," she wrote. "Also on the list was my book *A Wind in the Door*. I am totally baffled and frankly fascinated. This is the first time C. S. Lewis and I have been listed together as writers of pornography. I don't know whether to laugh or cry."[19]

In fact, the parallels between Lewis and L'Engle are striking. They shared the same birthday, for starters, November 29; Lewis was exactly twenty years older. They both wrote widely in many different genres, for both grown-ups and children, and are credited with influencing the faith of generations. However, they never met and inhabited vastly different planes of understanding the world.

When it came to a vision of the created order, Lewis was a Medievalist: for him, all creation comprises a hierarchy of beings, from stars to planets to angels to humans to animals and on down the list. And while this framework limited his imagination regarding such things as gender and societal roles, he insisted that every living person bears a "weight of glory" that would bring us to our knees in worship of them if it weren't for the mercy of God.[20] Madeleine, meanwhile, stressed that it's this very same love and mercy that makes equals of us all, women and men, children and adults alike; indeed, the suffering of the smallest mitochondria affects the farthest flung galaxies of the universe. She refused to accept traditional categories that would limit what is possible in God's world. Next to Lewis, Madeleine looks practically postmodern.

And yet Lewis and L'Engle were barely one generation apart. It's hard to believe she started working on *Wrinkle* a mere three years—*three*—after Lewis's final book in the Chronicles of Narnia, *The Last Battle*, won the Carnegie Medal in 1956. Yet both were, in their own ways, reacting to the assumptions of modernism, of the Enlightenment, which insisted that the only truths we can accept are those facts provable by science. To combat this, Lewis mined *back* into the riches of tradition—the ancient myth of Cupid and Psyche for his novel *Till We Have Faces*, for instance, or from Plato and Aristotle's universal moral law in *The Abolition of Man*—in order to glean insights about God and human nature that had been dismissed or forgotten.

L'Engle, by contrast, pressed *forward* into the mysteries of scientific discovery. As we'll discuss more thoroughly in chapter four, she engaged science in part to show just how small, how relative, how limited our view of God has been in light of the wonders of an astonishing universe.[21] Each new discovery doesn't diminish our faith; it increases our sense of awe that this same God, whose works are revealed to be more amazing by the day, loves us enough to become one of us and knows each of us by name.

Perhaps because of his mining back, Lewis was able to reach that generation of American evangelicals, those Baby Boomers and early Gen-Xers, whose parents and grandparents had lost their sense of wonder and yet still valued tradition. He gave those evangelicals the ability to say, "Yes, tradition matters, but you haven't gone back far enough. You must reclaim myth and mystery." But for many postmoderns, it's Madeleine—in her pressing forward; in her trust that ongoing scientific discoveries only bolster our understanding of God; in her "unwillingness to limit God in any way"[22]—who has become a bridge to Christian faith even more, perhaps, than Lewis. Indeed, one could make the case that Madeleine is the C. S. Lewis for a new generation.

She was, like Lewis, a lay evangelist—or more specifically, an apologist who attempts to explain the plausibility of Christian belief to skeptics and nominal believers. Her calling was, first, to those who don't know God in Christ. In the words of L'Engle scholar Donald Hettinga of Calvin College, "She perceives the mission of all Christians to be evangelical, concluding, nonetheless, that her mission is not to alienate non-Christian readers by antagonizing them."[23] One of her editors recalls, "In a way, Madeleine was always preaching: in her books, in conversation. She had a mission, and a part of the editorial work was trying to pare some of that down in her fiction."[24] This comment sheds even more light on the reaction of the publishing world to her overt Christianity, which was, how can we soften this, cut it down, if not cut it out?

Her calling as an apologist was, secondarily (and not because she wanted it), to the Christian fundamentalists bent on limiting God. Some have described her as even having a kind of "mission" to conservative evangelical communities. Says her granddaughter Charlotte, "I think she felt she had a real mission with what she called 'fundalits'—fundamentalist literalist interpreters of the Bible. She felt she had something to say to them."[25] To Madeleine, these were people that needed to be set free from binary thinking about how God chooses to engage the world.

But many conservative Christian communities she tried to reach were skeptical, particularly of what they felt were dangerous theological errors in her thinking. A signature accusation was universalism, the belief that, at the end of all things, everyone will be saved. She writes about being interrogated by a student at a conservative college during a Q&A session as to whether she was a universalist. She replied that she was not. But the student kept pressing her, insisting, "But your books do seem to indicate that you believe that God is forgiving."

"What an extraordinary statement!" Madeleine exclaimed.

The conversation devolved from there, with the student backpedaling a bit, and Madeleine pressing him, "I don't think God is going to fail with Creation. I don't worship a failing God. Do you want God to fail?"

Well, insisted the student, there had to be "absolute justice."

"Is that what you want?" she demanded. ". . . Me, I want lots and lots of mercy. Don't you want any mercy at all?"[26]

Luci Shaw too, from a much more loving stance, pressed Madeleine on the topic of universalism. Whenever Madeleine insisted that "no one will finally be excluded from the party," Luci pushed back: what if people *choose* to be excluded? Luci recalls, "We discussed this endlessly, for my part referencing C. S. Lewis's depiction of [George] MacDonald in *The Great Divorce* that ran counter to her conviction. I guess I came to think: 'Well, if universalism is a heresy, it's one I wish were true!'"[27]

Not all of Madeleine's detractors were so gracious. Confrontation after confrontation finally forced her to try and understand what evangelicals meant by the charge of universalism. Eventually, her interpretation was that "what the evangelicals mean by universalism is that all of a sudden, and for no particular reason, God is going to wave a magic wand and say, 'Okay, everybody, out of hell, home free.' So, no, I say, I am not a universalist; that plays trivially with free will."[28] This is not the sum total of what all evangelicals believe about the topic (and there's a ranging spectrum), but it was, for her, a meeting point.

But the damage was done. No matter what she said, critics insisted on seeing heresy in her writing. In an attack on *An Acceptable Time*, one of her detractors warns that L'Engle is writing a "recruiting manual" for druidism and New Age thought, making her "trusting young reader easy prey for Satan's snare."[29] And yet Madeleine's book depicts the main character, Polly, praying to Jesus, who "always was."[30] Polly is about to be sacrificed to appease the gods, but instead of giving into terror, "she was calling on Christ for help," repeating the fifth-century words of Saint Patrick: "Christ beneath me, / Christ above me, / Christ in quiet, / Christ in danger."[31] Polly is not saved by ancient druidism but by calling on the even more ancient, eternal person of God in Christ.

Yet for Madeleine, controversy was an unwinnable battle. When I asked Luci whether she got blowback for publishing Madeleine's books, she said, "Oh, yes. As publishers we went to the Christian Booksellers Association, which had a yearly convention in various parts of the country. And we would have a table with our books, with Madeleine's book, and people would come up to me and say, 'That's New Age. How can you carry that book?' There was a fair amount of prejudice against it in that area. . . . People said, 'Oh, you're making money out of the devil.'"

If these episodes were common—and irritating—for Luci, they were much more so for Madeleine. Such encounters were stressful and deeply saddening, and any one of us would be tempted to simply stop speaking at institutions where a fire of accusations could come hurling. But not Madeleine. Philip Yancey told me, "I had my own share of criticism over the years, and it's not easy to take. But here are people she has much in common with, and yet they're calling her a heretic or a witch and banning her books in libraries. And that hurts. It hurts at a deep level, and you have to come up with a way to deal with it. And she came up with a way." Madeleine continued, in her relentless style, to not only engage those communities but even found herself, at times, among unlikely friends.

●   ●   ●   ●

When Madeleine was still a young college student, searching for answers, "The first Sunday I went to church and nobody spoke to me, so I never went back."[32] Later she and her husband, Hugh, attended a Congregational church in Goshen, Connecticut, the location of Crosswicks: "In that church, we found friends who are still friends for life,"[33] she wrote. "I also learned why I am not a Congregationalist." Madeleine in time circled back to the Episcopal Church, and that's where she stayed.

Both C. S. Lewis and L'Engle had the knack for creating rippling rings of community and connection. They were friends with Christians, atheists, agnostics, and everything in between. Indeed, L'Engle, as a one-time president of the national Author's Guild Council, counted among her colleagues some of the household names in the publishing world, including authors like Judy Blume and Lloyd Alexander. And yet this world rarely overlapped with the Christian nonfiction she published with people like Luci, or the evangelical speaking circuit she traversed. Her secular colleagues knew she was a Christian, but the extent of her influence was likely underestimated— especially since the only Christians such mainstream authors tended to interact with were those fundamentalists intent on shutting their books down.

L'Engle sought sacred communities in her work with the Episcopal Cathedral of St. John the Divine in Manhattan as volunteer librarian and writer-in-residence. She also served as a writing instructor and retreat leader for the Community of the Holy Spirit, an Episcopal convent not far from St. Hilda's and St. Hugh's private school (where her children had attended). Later in life she worshiped at All Angels' Church on the Upper

West Side. These were sacred spaces, sacred friendships, particularly with Canon Edward West of the Cathedral until his death in 1990. His office was immediately next to hers; he was her adviser and spiritual director, a kind of father-figure, one of those rare friendships between giants in their own spheres.

But the Christian friendships didn't end there. In the mid '80s, author and spiritual director Richard Foster began gathering a group of Christian writers for regular retreats. In time, the group became known as the Chrysostom Society and went on to publish numerous collections together. "I think Madeleine found this was a safe place," Philip Yancey recalls of those early meetings, "a safe place where she could give her own opinions—and as I mentioned, they were strong opinions. She would say things like, 'I'm not a Christian writer, I'm a writer who happens to be a Christian!' But she was a Christian and she found some commonality, and I think she found genuine fellowship in that group."

The very first gathering on a snowy weekend in the Colorado Rockies led, rather improbably, to an uproarious serial murder mystery called *Carnage at Christhaven*. It features a group of writers, each of whom looks and acts suspiciously like a real-life counterpart, trapped together at—you guessed it—a resort in a Colorado snowstorm. Each member of the group took a different chapter, and no one knew where the story was going until the previous chapters were handed to them. Not surprisingly, the plot twists, devolves, revives, implodes—and it's hilariously, intentionally awful.

"I refused to cooperate," Philip remembered, laughing. "I said, 'I don't know anything about writing fiction, it's not a game. You need to know what you're doing.' And everyone else punished me by making me the [first] victim of the carnage of that book." In the opening chapter, a character dubbed Nathaniel Yates, "the writer whose several books had only recently made pain a popular topic of polite conversation," is found murdered.[34] Among the many suspects is Philippa d'Esprit, "an elderly Episcopalian, a prolific writer of adult stories for children" whom we first encounter sitting "erect, bejeweled, gowned in brocade."[35] She had grown irritated by the state of publishing; and "closing her eyes, she yearned intensely for the thirteenth century."[36] Chapters later, Philippa ends up nearly being wiped out by, of all people, her closest friend there—a seemingly gentle-souled poet who looks unmistakably like . . . Luci Shaw.

Welcome to your evangelical fellowship, Madeleine: they love you enough to fictionalize and nearly murder you.

●　　●　　●　　●

"In that curious and artificial divide between the secular and spiritual worlds," writes Luci in the foreword to Carole F. Chase's *Suncatcher: A Study of Madeleine L'Engle and Her Writing*, "there has long been a dearth of effective interpreters—communicators who can bridge a gap by planting a foot firmly in both worlds and representing each to each with integrity and enthusiasm. Madeleine L'Engle, as one such mediatrix, has made an astonishing contribution to contemporary culture."[37] Indeed, I would argue that perhaps more than any other author, Madeleine reached a new generation of wavering evangelicals and post-fundalits with a message of hope.

A few years ago I was invited to join a private Facebook

group of youngish artists, writers, and culture-makers whose experience with organized religion is rocky at times. Many were raised in conservative circles and have since moved left, either socially or theologically or both. Some have become Catholic; many have given up on church altogether. Some are attempting to speak prophetically to our evangelical communities, deeply troubled by the increasing polarization over politics, particularly in regard to issues of race, gender, and ethnicity. We lament the shrinking role of artists in faith communities; the collapse of discourse into blunt, graceless, unwinnable battles; and the inability of people on both the left and the right to laugh at themselves. And lest you assume we're overthinking all this, most posts either begin with or devolve into scatological humor or innuendo. Because if you can't laugh when the world is burning, you've lost your bearings.

It was to this group that I posed the question, "Who here can claim that Madeleine saved their faith/art/life?" And the responses kept coming. "She basically saved my faith after a bout with bad charismaticism," wrote one member. "Maybe not 'saved,' but radically changed; absolutely," wrote another. One person claimed that Madeleine saved her life "in a literal way," and then went on to describe a nervous breakdown interrupted by a flash of insight from *A Wrinkle in Time* (more on that story in the epilogue). Fascinated, I couldn't let any of these stories go. I had to find out more.

For Chris Smith, editor of *The Englewood Review of Books*, questions about his faith began after a transplant to Taylor University in Indiana from his home in Washington, D.C. "I moved five hundred, six hundred miles away from where I grew up," he said, "and, in a distinct way, uprooted myself from family and church and all the things that give meaning and bearings to our life." He began to turn away from the conservative culture of his home church: "Part of the struggle was disillusionment with evangelicalism," he recalled. "[Madeleine's] works were some of the first that helped me rethink some of those questions about who God is . . . The Genesis Trilogy, particularly, was really helpful to me, and realizing you could be a Christian and have deep thoughtful commitment to following Jesus outside of evangelicalism."

Smith was so influenced by L'Engle that he created one of the first websites for her fans in the mid '90s. It was through that site and its discussion forums that he met his wife, Jeni.

Jeni too came from a conservative background: "When I first read some of Madeleine's nonfiction and heard the term *fundalit*," she recalled, "I knew what a fundamentalist was, but I had never considered that that's how I had been raised. It seems obvious now, but it was all new to me." When asked for an example, Jeni explained, "My dad would decide he would take over the household finances because he was the man and that's what he was supposed to do. And we'd all be like, 'But Mom is the one that can do it; you can't. She's better at this.' And we all knew it." Jeni credits *A Live Coal in the Sea* as the book that sent her searching for others who were wrestling with questions of faith. "I feel like my faith is bigger because of her," she said. L'Engle challenged her to read Scripture as story and to see nuance instead of binaries, concepts that would've been heretical in the church of her childhood.

Religion writer Jana Riess remembers discovering Madeleine's fiction when she was a child, "and that's when I began to think a little more seriously about faith for myself," she recalled.

"I wouldn't say it was the only catalyst or anything dramatic like that. But it was definitely an influence, through her characters, that there were other kinds of Christian faith than the one—the pretty predictable one—that I felt was around me." For Jana, "church was part of the culture, people went to church, it was expected, it wasn't a source of excitement, spiritually or intellectually for people my age. And in her books you could see something so much bigger, so much more interesting and fluid and exciting."

Thomas Bona, a Catholic-turned-Mennonite from the Bronx, was introduced to L'Engle's work at a fortuitous time: right after the "first real challenge" to his faith. Though twenty years ago, the memory is seared into his brain. It was at a church camp during the summer between his freshman and sophomore years in college. One night a camp counselor spoke in tongues, placing his hand on Bona's head. The program director across the room began to translate. "She was saying things like, speaking as if the voice of God, 'Oh Thomas, you used to have so much faith, you used to believe so much, now you doubt. What happened? You used to be on fire for me and now you're not, and I can feel the flames of hell below us,'" he remembers. "I was paralyzed."

Thereafter he was torn by second guesses. If he didn't believe the way these faithful people did, he wondered, was he still believing? He grew to resent what happened. "Had those feelings festered, I don't know that I'd still be a Christian."

But then Madeleine intervened. A church leader lent him some books when he returned from camp, including the Genesis Trilogy. Bona appreciates L'Engle's "joyful uncertainty," he said. "She really wasn't like, 'here's why you should

be a Christian.' She was like, 'here's why I'm a Christian.'"
He can still quote whole lines from the book. The surprises
continued for him when he returned to Goshen College that
fall. "Madeleine was there waiting for me," he said. She had
come to speak. "I felt so blessed that God shared with me her
work that summer in a really painful, really vulnerable time."

●   ●   ●   ●

The more stories like these that I hear, the more I'm convinced
that Madeleine's mission as apologist to the wavering, the
wounded, the wondering, was a resounding success. She has
helped many of us cling to faith when our basic worldview
is being challenged by our own universe-disturbing questions.
She has encouraged us to rethink our theological assumptions
about what's safe versus what's sacred. She's challenged our
narrow reading of Scripture ("How does engaging this passage
as poetry, rather than as journalism, change the way I understand it?"). Even more importantly, she has kept many of us
from giving up altogether on the church.

But how did she, herself, arrive here? What steps in her
spiritual journey led to this unique approach?

Chapter Three

TRUTH *and* STORY

Stories, no matter how simple, can be vehicles of truth; can be, in fact, icons.

Walking on Water

Back when I was a full-time church youth director in my twenties, I could count on a panicked parent or parishioner approaching me annually, right before prom, with some flyer about "teen issues." "Why aren't you warning our kids about this stuff?" they would ask, "Why don't you teach a session on drugs and alcohol?" I tried to explain: Our teens were already overinformed. They were drowning in facts about sex and substance abuse—at school, at home, via targeted marketing—and these facts didn't seem to be particularly persuasive.

And anyway, why should "teen issues" be the only things youth supposedly cared about—issues, incidentally, that were not invented by teenagers? Why should their experience of faith be reduced to a long list of thin commands: don't drink, don't do drugs, don't lie, don't cheat, don't disobey your parents, don't have sex? As if a list of rules were the only thing our faith communities had to offer. As if rule-keeping were the only reason Christianity mattered, the only reason Christ died.

We have a better story to tell, I insisted. If we don't tell it, who will?

I never articulated my reasons very well. I didn't always convince even *myself*. There were days when I wondered, What if my job is to be like Ulysses sailing his crew past the Island of Sirens? What if the best I can do is tell everyone, "It's gonna get really bad. You're gonna really want to do something that's really bad"—then distribute earplugs and strap myself to the mast?

Nevertheless, I hosted book groups for middle schoolers in which we read things like *The Silver Chair* and *The Voyage of the Dawn Treader* by C. S. Lewis. Always in the back of my mind were the words of Madeleine L'Engle in *The Rock That Is Higher*: "Why does anybody tell a story? It does indeed have something to do with faith, faith that the universe has meaning, that our little human lives are not irrelevant, that what we choose or say or do matters, matters cosmically."[1] Ultimately, I decided, if I want young people to understand that their actions have significance, I'm not going to read kids a tract on substance abuse: I'm going to tell them a story.

It's what Jesus did with the parables, after all. "Who is my neighbor?" an expert in religious law asked him in Luke 10:29; and instead of listing five precepts about neighborliness, Jesus replied, "A man was going down from Jerusalem to Jericho . . ." Sermonizing on the topic would've bored his listeners and sent the questioner away feeling justified (the lawyer knew Scripture backward and forward already). But telling a story meant they would listen; it would lodge in their memories; they'd be mulling it over for days, months, years. Truth sneaks in through the back door of the imagination, while our defenses are down, when it has a greater chance of changing us from the inside out. *Let those who have ears, hear.*

Story, at its heart, is one of the primary modes in which God speaks to us. And thus it's one of the primary vehicles of God's truth. But it's also *formative* truth: the best, most ennobling stories have the power to shape our actions. "Rather than taking the child away from the real world," Madeleine asserted, "such stories are preparation for living in the real world with courage and expectancy."[2] The question is, where did Madeleine gain the wisdom and confidence to say such things?

● ● ● ●

I've already mentioned Madeleine's lonely childhood reading books and writing stories because her parents were so often absent. But Madeleine also claimed that "the greatest gift my mother gave me, besides her love, was story. She was a wonderful storyteller, especially about her childhood in the South. . . . 'Tell me a story,' I would beg, and my mother would take me in imagination back to her world so different from mine."[3] Before leaving for the opera, her mother would pause at bedtime and give Madeleine a bit of herself, a memory to treasure. Those stories shaped Madeleine's sense of family identity significantly and sometimes later resurfaced, fictionalized, in her novels like *The Other Side of the Sun* (1971). As a child, they helped her feel less alone.

At boarding school she was miserable and even "psychologically abused" by inept and cruel teachers, which is why, "possibly as a defense against the troubled, everyday world of my childhood, for nourishment I learned to rely more and more on the private world that I discovered in books."[4] Madeleine's maternal grandfather, who lived in Europe, regularly sent her English children's literature, which was unlike any of the forgettable things she was supposed to be reading for class. Books by E. Nesbit (*The Railway Children*), Frances Hodgson Burnett (*The Little Princess, The Secret Garden*), and Kenneth Grahame (*The Wind in the Willows*)—all nurtured her imagination, along with the Scandinavian fairy tales of Hans Christian Andersen and works by North American authors like L. M. Montgomery.

"I'm particularly grateful that I was allowed to read my Bible as I read my other books," she wrote in *Walking on Water*, "to read it as *story*, that story which is a revelation of truth. People are sometimes kept from reading the Bible itself by what they are taught about it, and I'm grateful that I was able to read the Book with the same wonder and joy with which I read *The Ice Princess* or *The Tempest* . . ."[5] She would later claim that she was grateful her parents slept in too late to take her to Sunday school; it shielded her from those well-meaning teachers who foreclose on—and even at times distort—what a Bible story means. (I say this as a Sunday school teacher myself.)

Her engagement with all of these books was deeply formative. They nourished "the same hunger in me, the hunger for the truth that is beyond fact, the hunger for courage and hope in a difficult world, the hunger for something more than ordinary vision."[6] But the one author who not only cultivated that hunger but fed her solid spiritual meat was the nineteenth-century Scottish minister and writer, George MacDonald.

Author of children's literature such as *At the Back of the North Wind* and *The Princess and the Goblin*, among other fairy tales, MacDonald saw storytelling as a moral enterprise: "In physical things a man may invent; in moral things he must obey—and take their laws with him into his invented world as well."[7] That's because the storyteller is not, ultimately, the source of storytelling: God is—and, for MacDonald, we cannot avoid accountability to the original Storyteller for the moral universe he has created. But that doesn't mean we bludgeon our readers over the heads with overt statements of Christian belief. MacDonald wrote in his essay "The Fantastic Imagination," "The best thing you can do for your fellow, next to rousing his conscience, is—not to give him things to think about, but to wake things up that are in him; or say, to make him think things for himself." For a preacher, this was particularly hard; MacDonald, throughout his fiction, seemed unable to occasionally refrain from sermonizing. But his chief desire was that "if there be music in my reader, I would gladly wake it."

And wake, it did. C. S. Lewis, for example, was in his teens, already an avowed atheist, when he picked up MacDonald's *Phantastes* at a train station sometime in 1916 and, a few hours later, knew he had "crossed a great frontier."[8] What it did to him, Lewis claimed, "was to convert, even to baptize . . . my imagination." The conversions of his conscience and intellect were to come much later; but the experience of "goodness" or holiness in the story—and the longing that sparked in him—was the catalyst for transformation. Lewis would go on to credit MacDonald for influencing everything from his understanding of heaven to his trust in the great love of God.

The same was true of Madeleine. In a little-known essay on the topic, "George MacDonald: Nourishment for a Private World"—which Madeleine wrote for a book with other members of the Chrysostom Society originally titled *Reality and Vision*, edited by Philip Yancey—she described how MacDonald shaped her understanding of God. MacDonald depicted God as "a loving Father who knows that sometimes 'No' is the only possible answer of Love, a Father who can be trusted, who understands laughter and tears, a Father who is nothing like the stern, Victorian image."[9] She also celebrated MacDonald's depiction of "wise women" such as the North Wind in *At the Back of the North Wind*, and the great-grandmother in *The Princess and the Goblin*, both of whom serve as mysterious, occasionally frightening, mentors and guides, much like the Holy Spirit.

So how does a lonely child come to understand that she is uniquely loved by God? That she, like each of us, matters? Through stories, Madeleine asserted. Through the writings of authors like George MacDonald. Through the kinds of books that she, herself, would go on to write one day.

●　　●　　●　　●

When I first began publishing my own books for teens on spiritual themes in great literature, it was because I had found so few resources out there. And no wonder. It's an embattled topic, as I learned the hard way. To wit, here's an early Amazon review of my book *Walking with Frodo: A Devotional Journey through* The Lord of the Rings:

Never in my life have I heard of such rubbish. The Word of God is to be the only basic source for the study of God's Word—not a trilogy of fantasy novels. Many Christians are becoming so wrapped up in pop culture that they have trouble differentiating the difference between the fictional events found within *The Lord of the Rings* and the true, inerrant Word of God. We need to get out of Middle-Earth and into the real world. You cannot find strength, guidance, and spiritual power in a fictional collection of stories, regardless of whether or not they are allegories of the Christian's journey. *Walking With Frodo*?! Is this meant to equate Frodo with Jesus Christ? Reality check: Frodo was never real, Middle-Earth was never real, and all the events which took place within Tolkien's world never happened. Christ was real, however. The battles He faced and the battles we face are very real, and we therefore should not waste our time in thinking that this garbage will assist us in them.

Pause. Keep in mind this sort of attack was par for the course for someone like Madeleine. (It also helped that other reviewers chimed in with everything from a thoughtful, well-researched defense of *The Lord of the Rings* author, J. R. R. Tolkien, to the obvious "Has the reviewer actually read the book?"[10]) I knew I was in good company, a literary tradition of readers and authors who—like Jesus with the parables—trusted the Holy Spirit to convey truth through the vehicle of story.

To understand Madeleine in context, as the direct literary heir of a particular strand of Christianity, let's back up a moment. Let's define what we mean by *story*—or, more broadly, *myth*—and how our understanding of myth shapes what we think about the claims of Christianity. I find it helpful to look at it from four views[11]:

View #1: All myths are untrue, including Christianity. This first view sees myth (cultural stories, legends, fairy tales) as humankind's attempt to make sense of a senseless world through sheer invention. This view is atheistic, existentialist: life has only the meaning that we bring to it. There is no inherent purpose to the universe: we create that purpose. Myths are unverifiable, unscientific, devoid of facts, and thus completely untrue. This view is also relativistic: if every worldview is essentially made up, then no one worldview or story is better than any other. In that sense, the Christian gospel is just another myth, lumped in there with everything else.

View #2: All myths are untrue; but the Bible is literal fact. The flipside of the above, one we've already heard expressed by my Amazon reviewer, is that everything *except* the Bible is false. The Bible is fact: it shares nothing in common with story or myth at all. Further, there is no truth outside of a literal reading of Scripture. Allegorical or even mythic interpretations of Scripture are therefore lies—or worse, deceptions propagated by the devil to drive us away from the truth.

View #3: All myths participate in truth; Christianity is no truer than any other story. This view—what we might think of as agnostic or "spiritual but not religious"—sees all myth as a shadow of the Real, an echo of the True, which remains veiled and mysterious. This view holds that most myths around the world share common themes (a creator, laws that must not be broken, a dying god), patterns that point to an underlying pattern to the human psyche that is both ancient and spiritual. It's a view made famous by mythologist Joseph Campbell in *The Hero with a Thousand Faces* and since embraced by many postmoderns. Like the first view, this one is relativistic: since all myths are attempts to articulate what psychiatrist Carl Jung called universal archetypes, no one myth is truer than any other—including Christianity.

View #4: All myths participate in truth, but Christianity is the Myth-Become-Fact. This final view of myth is the flipside of the above but with a uniquely Christian twist. It says that myths give us glimpses of a larger narrative that undergirds the universe: a story that will one day be revealed in full. Through the world's great legends and stories we catch hints now and then of what C. S. Lewis and his friend J. R. R. Tolkien called the "True Myth." For them, the veil over the Real has lifted, uniquely, in the person and work of Jesus Christ. The Mystery has taken on flesh and blood; the whole pattern and purpose to our human story has become known; myth has collided with history. As Tolkien wrote in his essay "On Fairy-Stories,"

> It is not difficult to imagine the peculiar excitement and joy that one would feel, if any specially beautiful fairy-story were found to be "primarily" true, its narrative to be history, without thereby necessarily losing the mythical or allegorical significance that it had possessed . . . The Christian joy, the *Gloria* . . . is preeminently (infinitely, if our capacity were not finite) high and joyous. But this story is supreme; and it is true. Art has been verified. God is the Lord, of angels, and of men—and of elves. Legend and History have met and fused.[12]

Before meeting Tolkien in the 1920s, Lewis had held the first view: myths were man's attempts to make sense of a senseless world. All myths, including the Christian gospel, were not true—beautiful, but not true. But then he met Tolkien, and slowly Lewis started to come around to the latter category. In Christianity, he realized, myth became fact. In a later essay Lewis summed it up like this: "The heart of Christianity is a myth which is also a fact . . . It *happens*—at a particular date, in a particular place, followed by definable historical consequences."[13]

This is the Christian literary legacy of which Madeleine was a direct cousin. Unlike Lewis, however, who converted rather spectacularly from atheism to Christian orthodoxy, Madeleine started out squarely in liberalism, a genuine seeker. "Myth is, for me, the vehicle of truth. Myth is where you look for reality. Myth is how God speaks to us . . . We do not say that myth is the truth. We say that myth is our striving toward truth."[14] Only in later midlife—through a kind of deepening rather than a conversion (as we'll explore in chapter four)—did she begin to embrace a Christ-centered orthodoxy, "the ultimate unfathomable mystery of the Word made flesh."[15]

She would go on to write, "If I speak of the Christian myth it is assumed not only that I am certainly not a fundamentalist, but that I am an intellectual who does not need God and speak with proper condescension of the rather silly stories which should be outgrown at puberty. But I am far closer to the fundamentalist than the atheist when I speak of myth as truth."[16] As with Lewis and Tolkien, she was intrigued by the idea that the best "myth" of all—the story that touches and enchants and changes us the most—became historical fact in

Jesus Christ. Jesus is not just any old hero from any old story; Jesus is wholly unique, the Savior of the world. His story is the True Myth. All the best stories echo the True Myth; and all the best mythmakers only do what they do because they are made in the image of a Maker who stepped into human history.

Madeleine wrote, "Jung says that we are a sick society because we have lost a valid myth to live by, and in my small back room I was absorbing a mythic view of the universe, a universe created by a power of love far too great to be understood or explained by tenets or dogmas."[17] For the writers of faith, this is how we give young readers hope that their small lives matter, "matter cosmically." This is our spiritual task.

● ● ● ●

Madeleine was turned off by the idea that faith can be reduced to a bunch of principles that intellectually must be affirmed rather than a Person whose Story and way of life must be embraced. Truth is not some abstract idea out there, as if we can divorce it from the story we inhabit as Christians, as humans. "It? *It?*" Madeleine demanded, "For truth we can read Jesus. Jesus *is* truth. If we accept that Jesus is truth, we accept an enormous demand: Jesus is wholly God, and Jesus is wholly human. Dare we believe that? If we believe in Jesus, we must."[18]

I'm reminded of the youth worker who pressed me, during a Q&A at Duke Divinity School about my book *The God-Hungry Imagination: The Art of Storytelling for Postmodern Youth Ministry,* on whether I believed in "absolute truth." Taken aback, I found myself insisting, "I believe in Jesus, who is the Truth." We volleyed a bit until the instructor (my good friend and colleague, Dr. Elizabeth DeGaynor) asked me, "Sarah, why are you being so slippery about this question?" to which I responded, laughing, "Because so was Jesus when Pilate asked him, 'What is truth'?" The youth worker—whose previous career, I later learned, was litigation—likewise laughed and said, "So, am I Pilate in this story?"

Many of us were taught that one must have a saving knowledge of Jesus Christ in order to be truly Christian, which involves assent to basic principles, agreement with certain "absolute truths," as the youth worker said:

God is the maker of everything.
Jesus is God.
He died on a cross and was resurrected from the dead
    for our salvation.
Confessing Jesus as Lord gives us forgiveness of sins
    and eternal life with God.
And so on.

These are all vital Christian beliefs. And yet, it's worth asking why Jesus didn't state them in exactly this way, over and over and over again, to anyone who would listen? Why veil them behind stories, hide them in parables, embody them in practices of healing, in miracles, in poetry like the Beatitudes, in cryptic statements that biblical scholars still can't quite explain? Why do we assume our methods for sharing the good news should be blunter than Jesus's own approach?

And meanwhile, many of us were also taught to view the imagination with skepticism. As Luci Shaw told me, when she first asked Madeleine in the late 1970s to write a book on faith and art, "There hadn't been much literature written that joined those two ways of thinking about life. And in fact, in those days, I think particularly in the Christian community, poetry was considered frivolous and not really worth spending time with. And it could lead you astray. I remember someone quoting the book of Genesis to me about the imaginations of your heart and 'all the imaginations of their hearts were only evil continually [see Genesis 6:5 KJV]'; so that was the context in which imagination was received in many conservative circles."

Visual artist Makoto Fujimura (*Culture Care*) told me, "Madeleine gave us the language to value imagination. That gift resonates in the gap between art and religion, but also for society at large." Indeed, the imagination plays a vital role in spiritual formation. Without it, we can't visualize the ancient world of the Scriptures; we can't grasp the metaphors of Jesus's parables; we can't practice empathy by seeing things from someone else's perspective, nor picture the people we're interceding for in prayer. We can't trace a pattern of meaning in the events of our lives, and we can't dream a better dream for the future God has in store. Someone might give us all the knowledge and information there is to know about Jesus, but it takes the Holy Spirit at work in the imagination to connect the dots to our real lives on the ground.

"When we try to define and over-define and narrow down," Madeleine wrote, "we lose the story the Maker of the Universe is telling us in the Gospels. I do not want to explain the Gospels; I want to enjoy them."[19] Those of us from Reformed backgrounds instantly recognize echoes of the Westminster Catechism, through which we were taught that the "chief end" of humankind is "to love God and enjoy Him forever." It's not, chiefly, to understand God. It's not, firstly, to get all our theology right. It's to delight. Love. Worship.

This can happen with the child alone in her apartment reading stories. But spiritual formation can't just be a private enterprise. As Madeleine eventually began to understand, it takes place best within the faith community as it gathers for its main worship service: through music, prayer, hearing or telling biblical narratives, testimony, creeds—all of which constitute a deep well that nurtures the human heart and imagination with meanings that may not be intellectually graspable. The mentally disabled kid in the front row can encounter Jesus while taking Communion even if he can't string together the words to tell you who Jesus is or what Jesus has done for us. We affirm the faith by participating in its communal stories together.

Madeleine also eventually recognized that simply hearing and telling stories is not enough. After all, it was her fellow Christians who were her fiercest critics, and hadn't they read the same Bible stories she did? Didn't they worship the same God? Madeleine began to realize that we can't neglect to talk *about* the Bible, *about* worship, *about* the key doctrines of faith as a way to help us articulate who God is and what God is up to. As she penned her various reflections on Scripture— things like the Genesis Trilogy, for example—she first engaged in wondering, then second, in stepping back to reflect. She said in *And It Was Good*, "I believe in the Bible as the living Word of God. But this faith involves an acceptance that the Bible is not static, that at different times the living Word can speak in different ways to different ears, and that even the Bible itself can never fully express or manifest the glory of the Creator. That does not make it any less the living Word. It is because it lives that it moves."[20]

Rather than jumping immediately to ideas *about* the Bible—say, three points about God creating the heavens and the earth in Genesis 1—she gave readers permission to encounter the story, to walk around inside it, to pause and wonder, to hear it in context. If we must extract three points from the creation account, let's at least refrain from announcing, "What the biblical author really means here is . . ." Really? We can say this better than the story itself? What if the story *is* what the Bible really means? The form of narrative carries the point and cannot be divorced from it.

It boils down to the question of whether we're comfortable—as Jesus was with the parables—in letting the story not merely deliver some other point but to actually *be* the point. When I ask my son, "What did you learn in Sunday school today?" am I expecting him to repeat some moral lesson about sharing? Or am I comfortable with him replying, "Once there was a man on his way from Jerusalem to Jericho . . ."?

In short, *do* I trust the Holy Spirit?

●   ●   ●   ●

Philosopher Alasdair MacIntyre, in *After Virtue*, wrote, "I can only answer the question 'What am I to do?' if I can answer the prior question 'Of what story or stories do I find myself a part?'"[21] Picture a teenager letting herself into the house after school. One text from her boyfriend ("can I come over"), and the narrative now can go several ways. But whatever she chooses will not be an isolated incident, as if this young woman only has a moral life when a decision faces her. What the next chapter of her afternoon holds has everything to do with the story that her life is already telling, the stories she embraces that have shaped her to be one kind of person over another.

Of what stories do I find myself a part? From birth we inhabit stories (usually more than one) that began long before we got here and will continue long after we're gone. We become part of narratives that are both spoken and unspoken, acknowledged and implied. And those narratives differ from family to family, community to community. How you act is influenced less by your acceptance of universal commands ("Don't get drunk") and more by the narratives your family or community tells itself ("Uncle Ron drank himself to death").

This is why stories get told and retold every year, every month, every time you sit down for dinner. Because it is through the stories that we learn who we are, what our community values, what our next line is supposed to be. "Deprive children of stories," MacIntyre says, "and you leave them unscripted, anxious stutterers in their actions as in their words. Hence there is no way to give us an understanding of any society, including our own, except through the stock of stories which constitute its initial dramatic resources."[22] In short, we are story-shaped people.

This point must not be confused with strict determinism, in which the odds are stacked against someone before she is conceived. It is not enough to tell young people, "Bummer. I wish you had been born into a different story." Such a response is on the same inadequate level as simply giving youth a list of bald commands and expecting them to be heroes in a moment of crisis. On the one hand we're saying, "You can't do anything about the story you find yourself in," while on the other hand we're saying, "There is no story except the story you choose when you have no story" (to quote theologian Stanley Hauerwas). In either case we have failed to offer an alternative narrative that has the power to transform the plot, the action, the script, the set, the entire stage of a person's life.

In her teen fiction, Madeleine was at times completely unsubtle about the kind of narrative forces that she believed shaped her main characters to act morally in the critical moment. In *Meet the Austins*, Vicky's grandfather, a clergyman, displays a poem on the walls of his loft, which Madeleine attributes to "Thomas Browne"[23]:

> *If thou could'st empty all thyself of self,*
> *Like to a shell dishabited,*
> *Then might He find thee on the Ocean shelf,*
> *And say—"This is not dead,"—*
> *And fill thee with Himself instead.*
>
> *But thou art all replete with very thou*
> *And hast such shrewd activity,*
> *That, when He comes, He says—"This is enow*
> *Unto itself—'Twere better let it be,*
> *It is so small and full, there is no room for Me."*

The poem gains in significance by the fourth book in the Austin Family Chronicles, *A Ring of Endless Light*, when Grandfather is diagnosed with cancer and Vicky herself attempts poetry of her own. Vicky learns that it's only in a kind of dying to self, of self-emptying (see Philippians 2:5–11), that we make room for God and others.

In example after example, Madeleine surrounds her characters with great literature, with quotes and songs from Scripture, with grown-up saints (flawed but not ruined), and with stories from history. She gives them mentors like Mrs Whatsit, who school them gently in a moral universe that requires certain actions if the story is to make the joyful turn. Madeleine gives them companions and guides—fellow teens but also key adults—who aren't afraid to affirm what is good and right in the main characters' essential nature and who hold them accountable to acting accordingly.

Here is an author who doesn't foreclose on what teens are supposedly interested in. Most of Madeleine's novels are family stories, for starters. Sara Zarr told me that, when writing *The Lucy Variations*, "I was very conscious that this was my 'Madeleine L'Engle book,' because it was full of classical music and adults. They don't break out into hymns around the fire, but it had that feeling of teenagers in a world of adults where there are a lot of adult things going on in a way I associate with L'Engle. That was my favorite kind of book when I was a teen, a young adult." Unlike contemporary YA lit, which often insists that young people prefer stories of teens operating in the world with no parental oversight, Madeleine gives us large families, tight-knit families, like the Murrys and O'Keefes. And many of their quests center around restoring family health and relationships, as in *Wrinkle*. While our culture assumes teens are interested exclusively in sex and social status, Madeleine gives us heroines like Poly O'Keefe in *The Arm of the Starfish* (her name changes to "Polly" in later books) who feel out of place for being nerds—and yet who are nevertheless affirmed by the adults in their life.

Meanwhile, many of Madeleine's male protagonists, such as fifteen-year-old Charles Wallace in *A Swiftly Tilting Planet*, are endowed not just with intelligence but intuition: they grasp they're part of a larger story that began long before they got here and will continue long after they're gone. When a crazy South American dictator threatens nuclear annihilation of the United States, it's Meg's mother-in-law who delivers the ancient prayer of Saint Patrick to Charles Wallace and calls him to act upon it. He eventually learns that his job is not to be the hero who claims victory through superior strength or even superior intelligence, but to give of himself for the greater good—to submit to a power of selfless love beyond his control.

Novelist and film critic Jeffrey Overstreet (*Auralia's Colors*) reflected with me on the tremendous gift Madeleine gave her readers by insisting on placing her characters in moments of vulnerability. "Charles Wallace and Meg are such unique heroes," he said, "because instead of building a strategy and arming themselves and marching on to war, they step into a place of vulnerability and uncertainty. And it is the love that directs them into those places that brings about healing, sometimes at great cost to them."

Jeffrey also noted how "ahead of her time" Madeleine was in the creation of Meg: "I think we cannot emphasize enough that she gave girls a protagonist, and not just a protagonist who is preoccupied with boys—although I do sometimes think that Calvin is a bit of an ideal figure. Meg has a maternal impulse toward her brother Charles Wallace; yet she's as capable with scientific concepts as any of the male characters." It's the creation of protagonists like Meg "that gives girls permission and validation and freedom to be themselves beyond the really narrow stereotypes that have been given to them, especially in fantasy literature."

But are these kinds of stories formative? Do they, in fact, shape young people to act in ennobling ways?

For author and blogger Sarah Bessey (*Jesus Feminist*), reading L'Engle coincided with when she and her parents first became Christians. No one else in the household was a reader, she told me, "so oftentimes I didn't have anybody to talk about those things with." She remembers reading *A Wrinkle in Time* "and feeling like it nearly broke my brain. But it just gave me such an expansive view of the universe and of physics and it seemed exciting and dangerous and had a lot of possibility to it." She would go on to read the rest of the Time Quintet: "I remember the meditations that Madeleine had on naming: it left a big theological mark on me, even as a junior high kid. I remember feeling the power of those words. It really deeply connected with the new things we were learning as Christians—because we were still very new to our faith as a family—about things like the power of your tongue, the power of your speech, why what you say matters in your life, and the things that you fill your mouth with and your brain with and your soul with *do* show up in your life."

More importantly, for Sarah, were the female protagonists. "It gave me permission to be smart," she said. "For a lot of us Gen-X girls coming up, a lot of that literature was really new for us, and so finding strong female heroines—that were smart and interested and empowered, had agency—gave me permission, whether it was implicit or explicit. And I don't know that

I would be the person I am now if I hadn't ingested a steady diet of all these fictional heroines who knew what they were doing."

For Jana Riess, the formative power of Madeleine's books came through a time of great personal pain. She was a teen when her father left the family: "He took my entire college savings, he basically took off and it was devastating. He left no warning, no forwarding address, he emptied out the bank account. It was a terrible kind of betrayal." She recalls the family trying to rebuild after losing everything, including his income—which meant they were plunged into poverty; her mother was now a single parent trying to make ends meet. "One of the books I read was *A House Like a Lotus* . . . a story of forgiveness, a story of how a high school young woman has her mind opened through a relationship with an older mentor [Max]. And this mentor ends up betraying her. I read that book over and over again. It was instrumental in helping me to forgive my father."

Several years later, when L'Engle came to give the commencement address at Wellesley College, Jana arranged to be her chaperone. "After this exhausting day where we'd picked her up at the airport and taken her to her book signing and then taken her to dinner, where she hadn't had a minute to herself, I basically followed her into her room with her suitcase," Jana recalled. "I'm sure that all she wanted was a moment to herself, but instead I said, 'I wanted to tell you how much that particular book meant to me and has helped me to forgive an adult who betrayed me.' And all she said—she kind of smiled and she said—'I had a Max, too.'" Madeleine didn't elaborate, but for Jana, "it was a meaningful moment for me to see the example of who she was and what she'd done with her life, and whatever betrayal had happened when she was young had not defined her."

For believers who pray the same prayers week after week, who come to the Communion table expecting to be changed, we must claim that it is possible for lives to be rescripted. We must assert that it's possible for habits and language to be reshaped by a different, more powerful story. The seeds for critiquing our behavior—indeed, for critiquing the tradition itself—are there inside the narrative we claim. The radical call of faith is not to insist upon a set of universal principles about right and wrong, but to offer an alternative story by which lives can be shaped into new instincts, new practices, new ways of speaking and being in the world. We want our teens to make a decision consistent with the better story of which they are a part, a decision that doesn't even feel like a decision but a script they know by heart.

●　●　●　●

I once heard a pastor contrast Ulysses's actions with those of Orpheus. Son of the muse Calliope and the god Apollo, Orpheus was the greatest poet and musician of Greek legend. Like Ulysses, he too sailed with a ship's crew past the Island of Sirens. But did he simply distribute the earplugs and hope for the best? No. The poet knew he could sing a more compelling song. He had a better story, a gift that would make the Sirens sound like the monsters they were. So as the ship passed the island, he played his lyre and told his tale. And the crew was so enchanted that not a man among them flung himself overboard.

Madeleine told a better story. This was her quest, to point others to the very same "light so lovely" that she herself had caught glimpses of through great literature as a child. Her stories were icons pointing to a source of truth beyond themselves and thus had formative potential for her readers.

But when, in her own spiritual formation, did she learn to call the source of truth by the name of Christ? At what point did her private enjoyment of God, while alone reading in her room, shift to communal worship with other believers?

Chapter Four

FAITH *and* SCIENCE

It was the scientists, with their questions, their
awed rapture at the glory of the created universe,
who helped to convert me.

Walking on Water

The summer between my junior and senior year of high
school, I attended a two-week arts camp at Adrian College
in mid-Michigan. We were an eclectic bunch: angst-ridden
poets, painters in tie-dye, nerdy novelists, the occasional pho-
tographer. None of us were angling for careers in science. But
one clear evening we were told the college's rooftop observa-
tory would be open later that night for anyone who wanted a
good view, through the telescope, of Saturn's rings.

We showed up in force. Maybe it was excitement about a
sanctioned late night out; maybe it was our longing for wonder. More likely it was the off-chance that a hand we hoped
to hold might be available in the dark. Whatever the case, a
line of maybe a hundred students slowly snaked its way up an
uninspiring cinderblock stairwell toward the rooftop, each step

lit overhead by ugly fluorescent lights and exit signs, all of us chattering at top volume about the usual nothings.

It was a long wait. Each student, we were told, would be given a minute to look through the telescope, and between each viewing the instrument's operator had to readjust it for the next person. To those in line, it felt like we were stuck in the stairwell half the night. But then it was my turn. One moment I was giggling with a friend, the next I was being summoned forth into a darkened dome by the instructor, who helped me onto a platform so I could reach the lens of the huge telescope pointed at a rectangular opening in the ceiling.

"Hurry," he said. "It's moving."

"What's moving?" I peered into the telescope. I'd imagined those close-ups of Saturn taken by NASA orbiters, the ones depicting a gorgeous ringed planet suspended in space, unperturbed and still. Instead I saw, 746 million miles away, a tiny white oblong, slightly stretched, with cartoon-like rings. And it was moving. No, it was zooming. It was hurtling in a straight, unrelenting line across nothingness.

"The earth is moving," the instructor said. "That's why I have to keep adjusting the telescope."

Suddenly my knees gave way. Underneath me the earth was spinning; it had always been spinning; we were improbably, impossibly clinging to a speck bombing through space. I was about to fall off.

He grabbed my arm. "Whoa, there! You okay?"

I nodded, speechless. He helped me off the platform. I stepped away, and it was someone else's turn. But returning to the stairwell and the fluorescent lights and the nonsense banter would be impossible now.

How could I have thought any of it mattered, any of those small, petty, wasted obsessions and conversations? How could anything matter again except the stark reality that my small earth, which held everything I knew and loved, was just one tiny dot, like that cartoon oval, hurtling through nothing? And yet my Christian upbringing had taught me that God made it. And further, God loved it and cared about its ultimate end. That he created and loved every one of us, loved all the angst and nerdiness and longing crammed under the exit signs. That he cared about me.

I didn't want to go back to the dorm then. I wanted to light a candle in a darkened sanctuary. I wanted to sing a hushed hymn under a vaulted, starlit sky. I wanted to write the story of such a cosmos, of such a God, forever and ever. Heading back to my room, surrounded by caterwauling peers—none of whom seemed half as awed as I did—I felt more small and alone, yet more significant and loved, than ever before.

Let's just say it was a Madeleine kind of moment.

● ● ● ●

"Wonder," says Hope College chaplain Trygve Johnson, "is the prelude to worship." No one understood that better than Madeleine herself. Her sense of wonder about the created universe began as a very young child, with one of her earliest memories:

I was visiting my grandmother at her beach cottage in north Florida. It must have been an unusually glorious night for someone to have said, "Let's wake up the baby and show her the stars." Someone came to my room, perhaps my father, and untucked the mosquito netting, picked me up, and carried me out onto the beach, into the night. And that was my first vision of night, of the glory of the stars, my first totally intuitive understanding that there is more to this world than the ordinary dailiness that makes up the small child's world, and where, as grown-ups, we are often stuck.[1]

Ever afterward she would say, "When my faith falters, when I feel God's absence, when I am moving through the night of the soul, if I can see a sky full of stars my heart always lifts."[2]

Anyone familiar with both Madeleine's fiction and her memoirs instantly recognizes in this early childhood experience the symbolic precursor to the "star-watching rock." According to her granddaughter Charlotte, there's no single rock near Crosswicks with that label; Madeleine used it to refer to any rock or outcropping from which you can watch the stars. Throughout Madeleine's memoirs she describes hiking to such rocks for solace, to unwind, to reflect. On one occasion, after a carnival in which some of the children had been given loud, garish toy trumpets, the family went to a rock, where they "welcomed the arrival of each star with a blast of a trumpet."[3] They were surrounded by singing insects with whom they joined in chorus, "outsinging them with all the nursery rhymes and songs and hymns we could think of which had stars and alleluias in them."[4] There it is: wonder, the prelude to worship.

In Madeleine's fiction, the star-watching rock, located in a field beyond the Murrys' farmhouse, is not only the gateway to wonder but also the portal to participation in the cosmic battle between light and darkness. It's even, as in *A Swiftly Tilting Planet* (1978) and *An Acceptable Time* (1989), the launch site for traveling to the past. In the opening pages of *An Acceptable Time*, Polly O'Keefe, Meg's daughter, makes her way to the rock, where she's startled to find the ever-angsty, boding-no-good Zachary Gray (who also appears, like Canon Tallis and Adam Eddington, in both the Austin and O'Keefe series). "It's a wonderful place to lie and watch the stars," she tells him, as if to assert the rock's true purpose over and against whatever romantic agenda he may have. "It's my mother's favorite rock, from when she was a child."[5] When, a few pages later, the rock is where Polly's time-traveling adventures begin, no one who knows Madeleine is surprised.

"The heavens declare the glory of God; the skies proclaim the work of his hands," says the psalmist in Psalm 19:1. Creation points to the Creator, and it's this God whom we worship. But it's also that same God with whom we have our biggest arguments, about whom we have our biggest questions. Does this God, in fact, love us? If so, why suffering? Why horrific brokenness and destruction, pain and death? Why such seeming abandonment? And why, oh why the flawed, awkward, insular, even at times hurtful community of people known as the church?

Madeleine may have grown up with an intuitive sense of God's loving presence, but her journey from solitary to communal worship was not made overnight. When her father died far too young, when she was just seventeen, her foundations were shaken:

I had not encountered a theology as wild and strong as [Saint] Gregory's when Father died. I had to struggle alone, and all I knew was that Father's death caused me to ask questions for which I could find no answer, and I was living in a world which believed that all questions are answerable. I, too, believe that all questions are answerable, but not in scientific terms, or in the language of provable fact.[6]

After a troubling conversation with a cynical peer, who questioned whether Madeleine's father did, in fact, still exist somewhere after death, she found herself affirming, or at least demanding, that we should not be abandoned by the God who made us. "I did feel, and passionately, that it wasn't fair of God to give us brains enough to ask the ultimate questions if he didn't intend to teach us the answers."[7]

Her Anglican upbringing had taught her to stuff her emotions, to press on without help; so she finished college and began writing, began working in theater, began dating. It was a tumultuous, crowded time: she was constantly surrounded by apartment-mates or traveling with theater companies. Late at night, she describes in *Two-Part Invention*, she would slip in the back of the Church of the Ascension at the corner of Tenth and Fifth (it was open twenty-four hours), just sitting and thinking, "not so much to pray as to take time to *be*."[8] But this was the extent of her churchgoing at the time.

Eventually Madeleine met Hugh, who himself had little interest in church after a conservative Baptist upbringing in Oklahoma. They talked about everything, it seemed, except faith. "We were articulate about the theatre, about books, about music, and amazingly inarticulate about our feelings."[9] One gets the sense that this remained the case throughout their married life, including when it came to Madeleine's insatiable theological curiosity.

It was after Hugh and Madeleine had married and settled in Goshen for that difficult decade of the 1950s—raising small children, running a general store, and struggling with her stalled publishing career—that her questions returned in force. The local Congregational minister (rather controversially, one could argue) not only asked her to direct the choir but to teach Sunday school. "I explained to the minister that I didn't really believe in God, but I couldn't live as though I didn't believe in him," Madeleine said in a 1979 interview for *Christianity Today* magazine. "I found life intolerable without God, so I lived as though I believed in God. I asked him, 'Is that enough for you?'"[10] Apparently, it was enough for him. She soon realized, through teaching teens, the inadequacy of trying to boil Christian belief down to a list of provable facts (trust me, sister, I've been there).

Her clergy friends also didn't dismiss her cosmic questions. In well-meaning efforts—after exhausting their own repertoires of responses, I'm guessing—they suggested she read the German theologians she would later deride for putting her to sleep. Whenever she humorously retold this story (it became part of her regular set list, cropping up in multiple books and lectures), she almost never named *which* theologians, exactly, although Rudolf Bultmann, Paul Tillich, and even philosopher Immanuel Kant are strong contenders. Madeleine fictionalized this experience in her 1982 novel *A Severed Wasp* featuring Katherine Vigneras (née Forrester, who had previously appeared in Madeleine's debut novel, *The Small Rain*, 1945):

[Katherine] repeated her bedtime routine, warm bath, slow drying, a book—not the mystery she was currently enjoying, but philosophy; Kant; she never got very far with Kant; the long Germanic sentences bored her, so that her lids began to droop. It was Wolfi [the nickname for her good friend, a Cardinal] who had first suggested using Kant as a soporific, "or almost any German theologian. It is said that we German theologians are the deepest-down-divingest, longest-staying-underest, most-with-mud-coming-uppest, thinkers who ever lived."[11]

Though Madeleine could laugh about it later, reading those theologians' attempts to define God and faith according to reasoned argument rubbed her the wrong way. "I asked questions, cosmic questions, and the German theologians answered them all—and they were questions which should not have been answered in such a finite, laboratory-proof manner. I read their rigid answers, and I thought sadly, *If I have to believe all this limiting of God, then I cannot be a Christian.* And I wanted to be one."[12] Like her character Katherine, "more mud was the last thing she needed. Theology was not helping her now."[13]

Meanwhile, she had begun taking an interest in the work of theoretical physicists. This part of her story, by the way, feels like the biggest non sequitur, and I'm not going to pretend it follows naturally from what we've understood about her so far. Was her interest sparked by the death of Albert Einstein in 1955 and the accompanying flurry of articles and commentary about his life and work?[14] Whatever the case, this sudden obsession became a spiritual turning point. "Einstein wrote that anyone who is not lost in rapturous awe and amazement at the power and glory of the mind behind the universe is as good as a burned-out candle," Madeleine wrote years later.[15] "I had found my theologian!"

Reading Einstein and others, she said, "opened up a world where I could conceive of a loving God who really could note the fall of every sparrow and count the hairs on every head."[16] She began to realize that if the Being behind the universe not only created and keeps track of every last particle but also loves this small planet enough to have become one of us, then Christianity was a faith worth claiming.

Madeleine was especially captured by the notion of "particularity," or what theologians sometimes called "the scandal of particularity"—that God chose a particular time (first-century Palestine) and a particular people (the Jews) and one particular man (Jesus of Nazareth) through which to enact the redemption of all things. "I believe that we can understand cosmic questions only through particulars," Madeleine said. "I can understand God only through one specific particular, the incarnation of Jesus of Nazareth. This is the ultimate particular, which gives me my understanding of the Creator and of the beauty of life. I believe that God loved us so much that he came to us as a human being, as one of us, to show us his love."[17]

It would take many more years before Madeleine recognized that embedding oneself in a specific worshiping congregation, with all its faults and inadequacies, is one key way of affirming the Incarnation. "If I go to services with reasonable regularity," she wrote in *The Irrational Season*, in 1977, "it is largely because I believe that if I am attempting to understand what it means to be Christian, this cannot be done in lofty isolation."[18] Worshiping God in the sanctuary of creation, under the vaulted sky, is powerful, yes. But we can't simply settle for generalities, forever only worshiping at no place in particular. Despite our frustration and disenchantment with human beings, eventually we must also take the difficult step of claiming a specific Body of people, with its unique grammar and practices, on one specific patch of earth—for better or worse. "So I go to church," she wrote, "not for any legalistic or moralistic reasons, but because I am a hungry sheep who needs to be fed; and for the same reason that I wear a wedding ring: a public witness of a private commitment."[19]

The scandal of particularity is what God's love looks like in person. We are, none of us, alone.

●　　●　　●　　●

Picture a campfire under the stars. Picture a harried mom stirring soup over the flames, one of ten thousand moms in a thousand campgrounds across Middle America. There's her husband battling tent poles (again) and their three complaining children, one of whom is perfecting the preteen eye-roll. It's the middle of a ten-week road trip across the United States— which probably sounded like a good idea when they first imagined it from the comfort of their country farmhouse back in Connecticut; but now, most days, it feels like an ongoing exercise in rage management. The mom retains her sanity by a quick walk to the lavatories beyond the ring of firelight while everyone is finally eating. She glances up at the canopy of galaxies overhead. Her heart leaps. Waiting for her in the tent, after everyone has gone to bed, is Albert Einstein.

Okay, so Madeleine's bedtime reading is not what I would choose on a family camping trip. By now we've confirmed that Madeleine was nothing if not entirely her own person. And insatiably curious. And, it turns out, this didn't stop once she made the turn toward Christian faith. By the late 1950s, she was firmly on the path of lifelong self-education that was nothing short of astounding—reading not only Einstein but also Max Planck, a theoretical physicist, as well as astrophysicist Arthur Eddington, for whom her character Adam Eddington is named. And many other scientists too.

When Madeleine and Hugh finally decided, in 1959, to move the family back to New York City, they first embarked on a summer-long family camping trip across the United States, which she fictionalized in the 1963 Austin Family chronicle, *The Moon by Night*. Her cosmic questions were still there. But now she had scholarly companions who didn't presume, like the German theologians did, to have all the answers. "In the evenings, in the tent, I read from the box of books I had brought with me: more Einstein; Planck, and his quantum theory; books on the macrocosmic world of astrophysics; books on the microcosmic world of particle physics. There I found ideas about the nature of being which stimulated and fascinated me."[20]

This was, for her, an "adventure in theology," a way to strengthen her belief "in a God who truly cared about every atom and subatom of his creation."[21] Partway through the trip, the names of Mrs Whatsit, Mrs Who, and Mrs Which popped into her mind, and a dim plot for *A Wrinkle in Time* began to form. When the family returned, she cranked out the manuscript in three months. It was, she famously claimed, her "rebuttal to the German theologians." It was also her "affirmation of a universe in which I could take note of all the evil and unfairness and horror and yet believe in a loving Creator."[22]

But the science in her books was not subsumed under this theological quest; indeed, her fans include many scientists who find her ideas compelling. People often asked Madeleine about her "great science background," of which she claimed to have none. She wrote in *Walking on Water*, "It has been a surprise and a delight to me to discover that my friends who are scientists, my son-in-law, Peter, who is a theoretical chemist, my godson, John, who is an immunologist, find the science in my fantasies to be 'real' and have passed them around to their friends."[23] A quick probe into science's response to Madeleine's work, more than fifty years out, reveals an ongoing and robust discussion.

Some hypothesize, for instance, that her ideas about time travel and the fifth dimension in *Wrinkle* could work mathematically, given some big assumptions. "The book talks about folding space and it talks about wrinkles in time—the idea you can take the dimensions as they are and change their shape," said astrophysicist Matt O'Dowd. To make that work, physicists use another dimension, the fifth dimension. "Adding another dimension potentially expands the realm of what's possible. . . . That's what Madeleine was getting at." O'Dowd compares Madeleine to other contemporary writers of sci-fi: "It's art meeting science or art inspiring science."[24]

String theorists—physicists whose hypotheses allows for up to ten dimensions—posit that if time travel were possible, a wormhole is probably how it would happen. A wormhole is a connection between two points in space-time, a theory

Madeleine uses as a narrative device in more than one book in the Time Quintet. Her depiction of tesseracts takes artistic licenses, but she gets credit for diving into a science that was only in its infancy at the time *Wrinkle* was written.[25]

Along the way, Madeleine admitted to being hopeless at lower math. ("Now, I understand that if I have nothing, and I multiply it by three, three somethings are not suddenly going to appear. But if I *have* three apples, and I multiply them by zero . . . why [are they] going to vanish"?[26]) When she discovered higher math, she said, she understood 0 x 3 to be "a philosophical, rather than an arithmetical problem"—which she then wrote about in her 1971 novel *The Other Side of the Sun*. Zero, she realized, was an annihilating power, able to "X" things in its path—a concept Madeleine continued to explore in *A Wind in the Door* (the 1973 sequel to *Wrinkle*). Demonic powers, or "Echthroi," engage in "X-ing" as a way of obliterating each living thing's created uniqueness, and Meg Murry learns that the only way to combat the Echthroi is by "Naming" what someone or something is, by stating its particularity out loud, by affirming that it's a beloved and irreplaceable creation.

Incidentally, the process of writing *Wind* didn't come easily. Madeleine claimed she had all the characters, but the story itself was not progressing in the direction she wanted. Then an old friend, who also happened to be a physician, sent her an article on mitochondria from *The New England Journal of Medicine*.[27] "Did that article ever disturb my universe!" Madeleine exclaimed. "I had never before heard of mitochondria. But I read that article and I knew that my book wanted to go into a mitochondrion. So I had to learn cellular biology.

I had to learn a lot more cellular biology than actually appears in the book so that the cellular biology that is there would be accurate."[28] It hadn't been until the late 1960s that the concept of mitochondrial disease and symbiosis were understood, said cancer researcher Natalya Pavlova, a L'Engle fan. By the time *Wind* came out in 1973, the implications of those new discoveries were still reverberating. "It's a very important [concept] in the book," said Pavlova, "that little components need to work together in symbiosis in order to make the world possible."[29]

"What appealed to me," said astronaut Janice Voss, of Madeleine's fiction, "was the sense that you just figure out what you need to do to solve the problem; and you use all the resources, and you pull all these interesting technologies together, whatever you can find, to solve the problem with the help of your family and friends." Voss explained, "And it was that combination of really focused problem-solving and a supporting team that's exactly what's in our space program today, as far as I can tell."[30]

For fantasy author Jeffrey Overstreet, the interaction of Madeleine's characters is precisely where science blossoms into theology. "She puts into the world of these very ambitious, very intellectual children these illustrations of wild scientific concepts," he told me, "and proves to you that there is no line between the physical world and the spiritual world, nor any division between the sacred and the secular. That what goes on in the nucleus of the atom is an illustration of what God is doing in the cosmos, and it's an illustration of love and the way we should relate to other people." He continued: "And then she illustrates in some of the most painful ways, especially in *Wind in the Door*, what happens when love breaks down at the cellular level."

But then, Jeffrey explained, the implications expand to the macro level. "It's an illustration of what happens in families, in churches, what's happening in America right now—that sort of withdrawal from other people because it's too risky. And it makes you vulnerable, and you put up your barriers, and then life starts breaking down." This is why Madeleine's heroes are so unique, he said (as quoted in the previous chapter). They don't bring about change by force, by blunt confrontation, but by placing themselves in a position of Christlike vulnerability. Love building things back up, from the cellular level, to restore the universe.

Somehow, a woman who had no formal training in either science or theology managed to bring the two into fruitful conversation. Rather than withdraw from either, out of uncertainty or fear, she pulled up more chairs at the table. And by doing so, she expanded our imagination of what God can do. "Madeleine-lightenment," Jeffrey jokingly called it, and he's right.

There's a lesson in that legacy. We have work ahead.

●　　●　　●　　●

Newbery winner Katherine Paterson (*Bridge to Terabithia*), in her introduction to the fiftieth-anniversary edition of *Wrinkle*, wrote:

> In our world, there are the scientifically minded that scoff at the stories told by the religious and the religiously inclined who refuse to accept the theories of modern science. The first group will wonder how a woman of Madeleine L'Engle's intellect could possibly be a Christian, and the

second will wonder how a *real* Christian could set such store by the words of Godless scientists. But Madeleine was, first of all, a searcher for truth, and so *A Wrinkle in Time* draws us into a new kind of thinking. Things are truly not simply what they seem in science *or* in religion. And if we graduate, as she did, from Newton to Einstein, we might discover that those two worlds are not as far apart as we imagined.[31]

Madeleine herself often said, "I've never seen any conflict between science and religion, because all science can do is enlarge our vision of God."[32] (I recently heard philosopher Peter Kreeft make a similar comment during his opening plenary at the 2017 C. S. Lewis Festival in Petoskey, Michigan: "No scientific discovery has ever refuted any Christian doctrine, ever, in the history of the world.") The conflict between those camps is perhaps too often overblown in public discourse, to all our loss.

This is particularly true when it comes to questions of human origin. When Madeleine herself was asked about creationism versus evolution, she just laughed and said, "There is only one question worth asking, and that is, 'Did God make it all?' If the answer is yes, then why get so excited about it?"[33] She then went on to explain her thoughts on evolution as a mode of creation, then concluded, "But if I should find out tomorrow that it all came about in a completely different way, that would have no effect on my faith, because my faith is not based on anything so peripheral. Thank God. If it were, I'd never have made it through the past year."

And she's right. None of us survives a tough season in life by exclaiming, "Well, at least I know God created the world in seven days!" or "At least he used evolution, by golly." Rather, we cling to something far more essential, the love and mercy of God in Christ, which began before any worlds were made.

Scientists themselves are often the first to tell us that science can't explain everything. Their discoveries are ever growing, expanding, fanning out like the universe itself (some theorists even posit an infinite number of universes); and yet even as new discoveries are made, science will always fall short of explaining what it's all here *for*. Not just what each particle does, but *why* a particle in the first place? Why the grand design? Why the anthropic moment, when the universe somehow, improbably, became able to support human life? And where is all this headed anyway?

Likewise, on the religious side of things, the Bible is not a comprehensive encyclopedia of data—nor was it intended to be. The first chapter of Genesis, for example, is a poem about God's creation of the heavens and the earth; the second chapter (also about creation) is prose. These are not two separate, even conflicting, "accounts," as they're so often called—as if journalistic reporting was a thing in the ancient Near East. They're two distinct literary forms meant to render a theological portrait—and what painter's style looks exactly like another's? Yet both are true in the sense that both are faithful to the character of God and God's intent in creation. Their genres, to a great extent, limit what each can include: for instance, whatever is included in Genesis 1 must fit the repetitive pattern of the poem. But each genre also comes with strengths: for instance, poetry is memorable precisely because it's repetitive— "And God saw that it was good." This theological refrain about the goodness of creation becomes unforgettably seared in our minds by the power of poetic structure. The details, for this poet, of *how* God created are merely ancillary.[34]

Such clarity about genre doesn't foreclose, however, on wondering about the Bible. In fifth grade I asked my pastor-father how dinosaurs could be possible, how the world could be so old when the Bible seems to indicate it's so young. He said something like, "Well, in the psalms it says that a thousand years are like one day to God, and a day is like a thousand years. So, God's way of marking time isn't limited to the way we think of it."[35] Since no humans were present during the unfolding of creation, I began to wonder, perhaps the best way the writers could depict it was in terms we can understand: days, weeks. Perhaps these were metaphors for the passing of time. Obviously, God could create it all in six seconds if he wanted to. Or six literal days. But the scientific record seems to indicate a much longer process. Whatever the case, I (like Madeleine) concluded, God did it. He did it all.

This seemed a reasonable, even obvious, stance for Christians to adopt. So when I toured Wheaton College as a high school senior and saw a large Ice Age mastodon on display in the science department, I thought nothing of it. ("Perry," it's called, and it's at least eleven thousand years old. The bones were uncovered nearby.) Of *course* Christians should celebrate the scientific discoveries from prehistory that expand our understanding of God's limitless creativity.

What took me by surprise were the anti-scientific, indeed, anti-intellectual Christians I began encountering in small pockets of conservative evangelicalism. In fact, when I took a creation-evolution class, our professor—who wisely never told us what he thought about the role of evolution in creation, opting instead to let us think for ourselves—told us there were parents who wouldn't send their kids to Wheaton because it didn't teach young-earth creationism (which posits the earth was created in six literal days and is roughly six thousand years old). Once again: a Creator who is known more by what he *can't* do than by what he can.

Maybe that's why I eventually chose a roommate who was majoring in geology and minoring in art. Chloe was an outsider, like me, except her difference was not denominational but regional: she was from the Northeast, where there were so few evangelicals that she'd had to go to another town for youth group. (On one of our first meals in the dining hall, she looked around at the mass of students and said, "I didn't even know there were this many Christians in the whole United States!") Meanwhile, she seemed completely nonplussed by any controversy between faith and science; she just went on studying rocks that were billions of years old and praying enthusiastically and painting lilies on huge canvases, and none of that seemed weird.

As a geology major Chloe had an almost childlike sense of wonder about the created world: "Wow, look at the atomic structure of this particular mineral—isn't God amazing?" I knew just enough science to know that I didn't *really* know what she was saying, but I could grasp the wonder. It was what I had felt too when reading fiction as a child, when encountering a particularly vivid character or snippet of dialogue or metaphor. It's what I'd felt looking at a distant planet zooming across the dark. It was this sense of wonder I was beginning to worry we'd be forced to grow out of, yet another line we weren't supposed to cross.

It seems natural, now, that Chloe was so drawn to Madeleine L'Engle. And she made sure I was too. Her Christmas gift to me in 1992 was L'Engle's *Ladder of Angels*, Bible stories retold by Madeleine and illustrated by children from around the world. It was Chloe's way of saying, "Don't lose that wonder. See? Madeleine hasn't! And look what she's doing." Twenty-six years later, I glance along my bookshelves and *Ladder of Angels* is still there, right next to *A Swiftly Tilting Planet* and *A Stone for a Pillow*. Do you know how many books I've gotten rid of in twenty-six years? But these I've kept, a reminder to not abandon the unquenchable awe of the psalmist, the scientist, the child.

●   ●   ●   ●

When asked what would be missing from Christian conversations today without Madeleine's influence, many of the people I interviewed for this book responded as Jana Riess did: "The fearless integration of science with fiction and the creative world."

Jana went onto explain that "Madeleine came of age as a writer in a time of modernism when there was this tremendous divide between religion and science, at least in the eyes of many people who were religious. Those were not reconcilable differences." Yet here was this Christian author who would throw some quantum physics into a novel. "That is a gift that few writers would have."

Jana recalled that when Madeleine joined Jana and her friends for dinner during the Wellesley College visit in 1991, the seventy-two-year-old author didn't simply dispense wisdom but expressed intense curiosity about all manner of topics. Jana's overall impression was that "there's so much that we don't know about God and the universe, its ontological essence, who we are, why we're here. There's so much more that we don't know than what we do. In Madeleine's work you get a sense both of the love of God and the infinite care that God has, this very personal care for every human being," Jana said. "But also a sense of humility, that we are not the end-all of creation; and when we think of something like a tesseract or just the constellations in the sky or quantum physics or all these things that she gets into in her books, it should be a very humbling experience."

Chris Smith of *The Englewood Review of Books* says his doctorate studies at Indiana University were influenced by Madeleine's mingling of theology and geometry. "The geometry we learned in high school is Euclidean geometry, which says that everything happens in a flat plane," he explained. "But Madeleine talks about if you take out the assumption of a flat plane and start looking at a curved surface, like the surface of a sphere for instance, then a lot of the axioms and assumptions we learned in a geometry class start to fall apart. But there's different ones that take their place, and you're able to develop a whole different geometry, a whole different way of talking about space." He was especially fascinated by its aesthetical implications, that there's beauty in a curved, rather than angular, surface—which, he said, also has theological implications, because "there's a connection between what's good and what's beautiful and what's true." That insight sparked his specialized course of study.

Not everyone has found Madeleine's interest in science compatible with Christian belief, however, and some even found it dangerous. One of her detractors wrote of tesseracts, for instance, "What she is introducing her readers to, in all reality, is known in the occult world as astral projection or astral travel."[36] In a satirical column "Open Letters to People or Entities Who Are Unlikely to Respond," published in the online journal *McSweeney's* in 2011, Natalie Grant wrote to Madeleine (who died in 2007, remember): "I know you got some Christian backlash because you wove so much science into your work. The loonies are still giving some authors a hard time, but no one handles it as gracefully as you did. To be honest, your view of God as someone who approves of time-travel and telepathy rocks my socks."[37] Natalie writes this tongue-in-cheek, of course, conflating science with science fiction, but she highlights the unhappy battle in which Madeleine was continuously embroiled with her ever-suspicious conservative critics.

Candy Bryant, a bookstore manager in Ludington, Michigan, said she thought she'd lost a customer's confidence about buying *Wrinkle* to read with her granddaughter because Candy waxed too enthusiastic about its mixture of science and fantasy. The woman's face fell; the customer mumbled that perhaps the Chronicles of Narnia would be a better fit. "I realized how in this political world people strive to put things in boxes, mark them 'safe' and 'unsafe,'" Candy reflected. "Something I said might have marked *Wrinkle* as unsafe for her. But I didn't want to make the book feel too safe for her. Good fiction, like life, is by merit unsafe." Candy was thankful the woman returned when the book order came in, read *Wrinkle* with her granddaughter, and raved about it.

But just the mere fact that Candy would pause, that her trigger response to a hesitant customer was fear that any mention of science might turn the woman off, shows just how fraught this topic is in our public discourse.

Perhaps that's why one of my favorite moments in my interview with Luci Shaw was her description of attending a conference with Madeleine in Cambridge, England, where Luci found herself seated at dinner between Madeleine on one side and theoretical physicist John Polkinghorne on the other. Polkinghorne is not merely a scientist who happens to be a Christian, but he's also an Anglican priest, a fact that must have thrilled Madeleine enormously. He's famous for that same "fearless integration" of faith and science as Madeleine herself—but he's just so twinkly and jovial and British about it that you can't be offended if you try. According to Polkinghorne (whom I can't bring myself to call "John"):

> Most of the great pioneer-figures of science were people of faith. And they liked to say that God had written two books: the book of nature and the book of Scripture. You should read both of those books, because God had written them. And if you read them aright, you would find that they did not contradict each other, because of course they had the same author. . . . [For instance] there are clear signs written in the book of nature, for all who wish to read, that the earth has had a long history . . . [it's a book] written by God, God who is the God of truth, and does not mislead those who read what he has written in the created order of the world.[38]

He's equally articulate about the book of Scripture, saying, of Genesis 1, "We are not reading some scientific text kindly provided by God to save us the trouble of actually doing science, we are reading something more profound, more interesting, more important than that; we are reading a theological text." Leave it to a theoretical physicist to clearly explain why literary genres matter.

So, there was Luci, the poet, seated between the scientist and the storyteller. I tried visualizing that tableaux.

"Oh, *wow*, Luci . . . ," I said, at a loss for words.

"The conversations were not just chitchat; they were expressing such amazing truths and discoveries!" Luci exclaimed.

"You mean you didn't sit there talking about the weather?"

She was laughing now. "Or the traffic!"

"I'd expect nothing less from that triad."

What an iconic image of the relationship between faith, fiction, and science—mediated by poetry, no less! (Am I the only one picturing Andrei Rublev's fifteenth-century icon of the three angels visiting Abraham in Genesis 18? No?) And what a vision, what a challenge for my generation: to ignore those social media algorithms that label and isolate, and to instead intentionally foster conversations, over dinner, with unlikely guests. That's the sort of conference we should all want to attend—and if we can't find one, we should convene it.

● ● ● ●

Only on Madeleine L'Engle's website would there be a blog post from her granddaughters about the annual Perseids meteor shower. "For her, stars were 'an icon of creation,'" writes Charlotte, "meaning that they helped her trust in God's love and the significance of an interconnected universe."[39]

In Madeleine's faith, stars literally were "a light so lovely," pointing to a truth, a Presence, greater than themselves. Again: not an idol that one worships but an icon, a window through which we can see the God who created all things.

And that, for Madeleine, is key. To force the claims of Christianity to rest on indisputable proof is to treat science itself as a kind of idol, the standard by which we measure everything. Then, when science seems to contradict what we thought Scripture was saying, our faith falters. But there are spiritual truths "beyond provable facts," as Madeleine was fond of saying, otherwise we wouldn't need faith for them. There are spiritual realities that science will never be able to prove, one way or the other—no more than anyone can scientifically prove that I love my husband.

However, when scientific discovery is treated as an *icon*—as a window whereby more of God's light and truth is illuminated—we can reenter the realm of childlike wonder and say with the psalmist,

> When I consider your heavens,
>> the work of your fingers,
> the moon and the stars,
>> which you have set in place,
> what is mankind that you are mindful of them? . . .
> . . . Lord, our Lord,
>> how majestic is your name in all the earth!
>> **Psalm 8:3–4a, 9**

Scientific pursuit, then, becomes a key spiritual discipline— a gateway, the prelude, to worship. I would go so far as to say that the study of created things can school us in wonder better than any other discipline. In what ways can we, like Madeleine, become lifelong learners? When was the last time you looked up at night, while walking the dog or taking out the recycling, and tracked the progress of a satellite? Are you sure it wasn't the International Space Station? (Who's all up there these days? What are they doing?) And what *is* the annual Perseids meteor shower, anyway?[40]

Meanwhile, technology in the service of science shows no signs of slowing down: artificial intelligence is being "trained," even now, to do everything from drive our cars to diagnose our illnesses. An idol in the making, perhaps, and what is far too quickly idolized can also become demonized—or worse yet, weaponized. By that light, holding faith and science together, as we move into the future, is a key Christian practice that we dare not dismiss or ignore. If I'm not training my children in the kind of humility and wisdom that recognizes both the dangers and the gifts of human knowledge, then I'm failing to equip them for faithful discernment. And Madeleine taught us how.

This wasn't the only spiritual practice by which she taught us well, however—nor even for which she is best known. We now make the turn toward Madeleine's commitment to yet another Christian practice, the vocation of the artist, and how that commitment has transformed a generation of writers and beyond.

Chapter Five

RELIGION
and ART

If it's bad art, it's bad religion, no matter how pious
the subject.

Walking on Water

For the past few years I've served as a preliminary fiction judge for *Christianity Today* magazine's annual book awards. Upwards of forty books—nominated by a dozen or so religious publishing houses or imprints—are delivered to my door annually in early August, and I'm given mere weeks to narrow the field. First I sort by genre (historical romance, suspense/thriller, family drama, biblical fiction, contemporary romance, Amish everything, etc.), then by writing style or literary merit, and occasionally by "I'm not sure what this is, but I'm intrigued." Usually it takes me only a few paragraphs to discern whether a book has potential, at which point I'll either sort it into the "No" category or read a bit further. If all goes well, I read the entire thing. In the end, I select four finalists, which are sent along to a quartet of final judges to pick the winner.

What kinds of criteria shape my decisions? Initially I struggled to define this. Was I merely favoring my personal preferences (for British detective novels, say)? Was it really fair for a grumpy English major to impose her tastes on an industry that never intended to cater to her tribe in the first place? Over time I realized I was operating by a perfectly valid set of intuitive criteria formed over many decades of being a reader, an author, a trained theologian, a fiction writer, and an editor of literary anthologies. This wasn't a matter of mere temperament. So I wrote my criteria down. I began to plant my flag in the kinds of terrain I think Christians, of all people, should be exploring— things I was seeing far too little of in the books that came my way. Here's what I've circled back to, time and time again:

- Excellent writing
- Complex characters
- Compelling plotlines and reveals
- Questions of ultimate meaning (or was this just a cute, entertaining love story?)
- Theological depth (or did the author fail to reckon with the problem of evil? of suffering?)
- A strong sense of faith communities as a vital presence in the world (or were churches only depicted as irrelevant, at best; or, at worst, dangerous?)
- And finally, global/cultural awareness (or did the author assume that his or her nationality, race, and class were normative for how the rest of the world should function?)

In other words, I grade on a L'Engle-inspired curve.

• • • •

So, what's an author's secret sauce? How does the magic happen? For Madeleine, what were the signs of greatness? It certainly wasn't hitting all my criteria, in every book, every time. Children's literature scholar John Rowe Townsend described Madeleine as "a curiously-gifted, curiously-learned, curiously-imperfect writer,"[1] and obviously, we can point to moments where any one of Madeleine's novels actually fail my bulleted list:

Excellent writing. Her opening sentence of *A Wrinkle in Time*, for instance, "It was a dark and stormy night," has appalled the literati for decades (so cliché! what is she *doing?*). Sure, great authors can get away with breaking rules, while the rest of us are exhorted only to do so in moderation. But was this one of those moments?

Complex characters. Meg Murry of *Wrinkle* is one of the best-loved female protagonists in the history of children's literature; yet at times the Murrys, Austins, and O'Keefes seem too good to be true. Writes Natalie Grant in her satirical letter to Madeleine for *McSweeney's*:

> Did you write [*A Ring of Endless Light*] just for me? I'm sure you did, because I was Vicki [sic] Austin. I, too, had the older brother, the dog, and the rampant transcendentalist tendencies. My family, too, was musical and nerdy-smart and pensive . . . we'd all sit on the porch in the evenings and talk about world issues, too! I could communicate with dolphins, too! . . . Well, except for a few minor details, you really were dead on there.[2]

One of Madeleine's editors, Sandra Jordan, said she told Madeleine in early drafts of *A Ring of Endless Light* that Vicky Austin was "so self-righteous that she came across to the reader as unsympathetic and smug."[3] So Madeleine made changes. Even Newbery Award–winning authors must attend to their characters.

Compelling plotlines and reveals. Madeleine's plotlines are occasionally stronger than the characters who inhabit them. *A Swiftly Tilting Planet* comes to mind, with its tight structure based on the lines of an Irish rune but its otherwise underdeveloped supporting characters from a dizzying range of historical contexts. Madeleine simply didn't have the space to develop all those personas. While reading back through her YA books recently, I was also struck by how often she rewards her teen heroines with what Jeffrey Overstreet calls "trophy boyfriends": basketball star Calvin O'Keefe to Meg, handsome researcher Adam Eddington to Vicky—heck, generally no fewer than three potential guys for Vicky, in any given book. That was certainly not a plot device in my own nerdy adolescence . . . and perhaps just the teensiest bit of wish-fulfillment fantasy on her part?

It's when we dive into the next few bullet points of my criteria that Madeleine really begins to shine:

Issues of ultimate meaning. Indeed, it's hard to find a YA author who beats Madeleine at addressing issues of ultimate meaning. Questions of origin (How did all of what we see in the universe come together?); questions of theological anthropology (Who are human beings? Who made us?); questions of purpose (Why are we here? Where is our story headed?)—back to Madeleine's own "cosmic questions." In her presentation by that title to the 1996 Festival of Faith and Writing at Calvin College, she said, "We read stories, and we write stories because we ask the big questions to which there are no finite answers. We tell stories about people who give us our best answers, in the way that they live and work out their lives and treat other people and try to find the truth."[4] If a novel isn't about those questions, then what is it doing?

Theological depth. Beyond issues of ultimate concern, she also expressed a theological framework consistent with the Anglican tradition: "Christ, the Second Person of the Trinity, Christ, the Maker of the universe or perhaps many universes, willingly and lovingly leaving all that power and coming to this poor, sin-filled planet to live with us for a few years to show us what we ought to be and could be. Christ came to us as Jesus of Nazareth, wholly human and wholly divine, to show us what it means to be made in God's image."[5] As we'll discuss further in chapter seven, she affirmed that sin is real and not only manifests in evil systems at war with God but cuts through every human heart. Yet God is intimately involved in redeeming human history—redeeming each human life, indeed, all of creation—through the incarnation, life, death, and resurrection of Jesus.

Granted, one could make the case that at times Madeleine drifted outside of orthodox theological bounds. I myself am troubled—when reading *A Swiftly Tilting Planet*, for instance—by what seems like her belief in fate and, on occasion, a vague form of reincarnation: that some genetic quirks have spiritual significance (close-set eyes, bad; clear blue eyes, good) and turn up every generation or so, for better or worse. Thankfully, someone like Charles Wallace can be tasked with breaking the cycle, a holy interference that points to a grace that overrides fate. But the reader is left with the sense that our lives and stories are largely pre-scripted; we are fated to speak and act in particular ways, even those of us who are ostensibly there to change the story for the better.

When Madeleine drifts into these sorts of speculations is when I feel her writing is at its weakest: an otherwise robust theology subsumed for the sake of a plot device. And yet, such instances are rare. More common—and more compelling—is her relentless insistence on the uniqueness of Christ, on the power of the Incarnation to overturn every device of evil, and "the basic truth for me, the freeing truth, is God's love, God's total, unequivocal love."[6]

A strong sense of the church and faith communities as a vital presence in the world. Here also, Madeleine's novels are unique. Yes, there are times when Madeleine paints institutional religion with negative brushstrokes—the witch-hunting Puritans in *A Swiftly Tilting Planet*, for example; or the demonically controlled canon of an urban cathedral in *The Young Unicorns* (which, I'm guessing, was her way of poking fun at her good friend Canon West). But otherwise, clergy like Vicky Austin's grandfather make regular, normal appearances. The families participate in worship; they include hymns in their singing repertoires; even angelic beings such as the centaurs on the planet Uriel in *Wrinkle* sing passages from Isaiah 42:10–12.

Global/cultural awareness. My final criterion is a bit trickier. On the one hand, Madeleine takes her predominantly white characters all over the globe (all over the universe, for that matter), to places such as an invented island off the coast of

Spain in *The Arm of the Starfish* and the jungles of Venezuela in *Dragons in the Waters*. Her engagement with other cultures, such as the native peoples in *A Swiftly Tilting Planet*, on the whole expresses a deep respect for their religions, for their relationship to nature, for their ways of life. But it's often a highly idealized view, born out of a kind of unrecognized privilege and white obliviousness that at times makes me cringe.

Taken individually, each of Madeleine's books could be said to fail somewhere. That's because she was, like the rest of authors throughout time, an imperfect human being whose greatness as an artist nonetheless somehow survived her quirks. No author or book is perfect. This is good news for the rest of us: freedom to be imperfect is a liberating force for any vocation. But for Madeleine, her greatness as a writer was bound up in so much more than words on a page. It was bound up in a whole life, in her influence on generations of other artists as mentor and guide. It's to that legacy that we now turn.

● ● ● ●

Almost immediately upon Madeleine's success with *Wrinkle* in 1963, the world wanted to know her secret sauce. She had already been teaching writing at her children's private Episcopal school, St. Hilda's and St. Hugh's on the Upper West Side, but now her role as popular speaker and writing instructor launched in earnest.

At first she ran the usual circuit of libraries and schools alongside such authors as Lloyd Alexander (the Prydain Chronicles) and Sidney Offit (*Memoir of the Bookie's Son*).

Offit, for instance, recalled the first time he and Madeleine were to speak together on the annual fall children's book festival tour in the 1960s. He had developed an entertaining style for children, while the more famous authors always seemed to him to be "deadly dull"—so he suggested to the host librarian that maybe Madeleine should go first, then himself, in case someone needed to salvage things after her presentation. "I can tell that you've never heard her speak," the librarian told him. "Don't worry about Madeleine L'Engle." Sure enough, Madeleine held the audience enrapt, like the trained actress she was.[7]

Her reputation as a presenter grew, leading to everything from teaching writing workshops in East Harlem to preaching at the Cathedral of St. John the Divine—where one parishioner considered her "the greatest preacher he had ever heard," with sermons that "were always captivating and original and yet informed by a powerful understanding of classic religion."[8] By the 1970s she was regularly leading spiritual retreats and teaching writing workshops, particularly through an Episcopal convent known as the Community of the Holy Spirit on the Upper West Side. She also added places like Wheaton College and many other religious institutions to her speaking circuit—when she wasn't doing things like addressing the Library of Congress, where she delivered her speech "Do I Dare Disturb the Universe?" in 1983.

In widowhood, during the 1980s and '90s, Madeleine increased her role as a writing instructor and mentor as well as spiritual director for hundreds of acolytes—most of them women. The smaller class sizes and intimacy of her workshops meant that many of them felt they knew Madeleine deeply and personally. Dinner parties and reunions at her Manhattan apartment became a regular fixture amongst her alumni, as described in their 2009 collection *A Circle of Friends: Remembering Madeleine L'Engle.*

One former student, Lesa Rader, told me, "I didn't feel that I belonged in that group of writers, but Madeleine made me feel that I belonged. She was authentic and a deep reader of the Bible. She also understood the pain and suffering in the lives of the participants." Lesa recalled, "At that time I was coming to accept my role as a parent of a child with severe disabilities, with all the guilt that goes with that role. She just accepted me and encouraged me to write about my experiences even more." Story after story by Madeleine's students reflect a similar attention to their unique circumstances.

Barbara Braver—who was Madeleine's apartment-mate for twelve years while commuting from Massachusetts to work part of each week in New York—said of those mentoring relationships, "Madeleine took very seriously the fact that she had a gift to offer and she offered it. She had the gift of drawing out of people their stories and encouraging them and prompting them." Barbara reflected, "Madeleine was also curious about people and relationships. And certainly, when you're talking to people about their writing, you're meeting people beyond their favorite flower and whether they like breakfast. That was important to her."

Of that circle, one of Madeleine's nineteen goddaughters, Cornelia Duryée Moore, became Madeleine's personal assistant and honorary family member. When Madeleine grew increasingly overwhelmed by the vast and echoing Cathedral of St. John the Divine, Cornelia says she persuaded Madeleine to join her in worship at All Angels' on the Upper West Side.[9] At Madeleine's prompting, Cornelia eventually went on to become a filmmaker, with collaboration from the author to adapt several of her novels and unpublished plays for film. *Camilla Dickinson*, a lovely, quiet film starring Adelaide Clemens and Cary Elwes (yes, Westley from *The Princess Bride!*), released from Kairos Productions in 2012, based on Madeleine's 1951 novel. The author never had the chance to see the production, obviously, but the two women remained extremely close (Cornelia's sons, Tallis and Theo, are named for characters in Madeleine's novels) until Madeleine's death.

The author's influence wasn't limited to her writing students, however. In 1979 Madeleine sat down with TV producer Norman Lear's young assistant, Catherine Hand, who from childhood had longed to see *Wrinkle* adapted for the big screen. Madeleine initially resisted the idea, but she and Catherine struck up a friendship that, for Catherine, became one of the most transformative relationships of her life. "Without question, Madeleine influenced my view of Christianity, God and the universe," Catherine told me in her interview for this book. "Madeleine and I developed a very strong bond over the years, and her trust in me mattered a great deal. I wouldn't give up on the film, because I didn't want to let her down."

The two would collaborate on how best to turn the book into a film. Their discussions led Catherine to eventually make a Disney television movie that aired to mixed reviews in 2004, and later the 2018 blockbuster produced by Catherine and directed by Academy Award–nominated filmmaker Ava DuVernay. For Catherine, the spiritual journey of having

Madeleine as a mentor was just as important as the collaborative result: "The most important thing a mentor can do is believe in you with their whole heart. I felt that from Madeleine, and I wanted to live up to the faith she had in me."

In the course of researching this project, I asked my peers and colleagues to describe the mentoring role Madeleine played, through her books, in their lives. When I asked them which title had the biggest impact on their faith or vocation, the 1972 Crosswicks journal *A Circle of Quiet* came up repeatedly: a book about finding the space to simply *be* without abandoning the tasks you're called to do.

Madeleine describes her difficult decade of trying to write while parenting small kids—which, for many women writers, in particular, resonates powerfully. Freelancer Aleah Marsden told me, "She blessed my desire to pursue something outside of mothering in a way that didn't diminish either calling's importance. Yes, of course, I was to be the best mother I could be to the children entrusted to me. No, they didn't have to be the epicenter of my existence. Yes, my writing was a gift worth protecting and pursuing, and I would be a better human (and mother) for it. No, it didn't give me license to abandon the embodied work that came with the season of mothering young children."

Missional activist D. L. Mayfield (*Assimilate or Go Home*) reflected with me, "Parenting small children both makes me numb and also causes me to turn over the biggest questions of all as I rock my children to bed or seek nurturing, wise books to read to them at night." For Mayfield, "Parenting has made me eschew religiosity in exchange for a real relationship—full of questioning—of a God I hope is more loving than I can possibly imagine. I don't think we talk often enough about how children both make it essential and impossible to write. Madeleine for me is a patron saint of this."

Author and blogger Sarah Bessey told me that reading Madeleine's description of the "tired thirties" was a tremendous encouragement during a similar stage in her own life. "Madeleine mentions that she used to literally fall asleep with her head on the typewriter. And at that exact moment I had just signed my first book contract for *Jesus Feminist*; I'd had three children in four years," Sarah said. "I was on maternity leave, and I remember the day I read that part of *A Circle of Quiet*: I was sitting cross-legged in the bathroom typing on my laptop, and the baby was having her nap, and I was still lactating, and I had my two other ones in the bathtub right beside me so they could be busy and have fun and be contained. And I had one eye on them to make sure nobody slipped under, and I've got the baby sleeping, and one eye on my laptop—at the same time I'm trying to write down some really big thoughts on patriarchy."

The biggest takeaway from Madeleine, for Sarah, was the idea that "just because it's hard doesn't mean you quit. Just because it doesn't look like everyone else's day when they're on maternity leave, or just because it's not this mythic, housewifely ideal that people like to have . . . if Madeleine L'Engle was just this tired and still kept going and fell asleep on the typewriter, then you know I get to keep going too." Sarah concluded, "It gave me permission to write that book."

It turns out, the secret sauce to great writing isn't some magic formula, but rather, it's perseverance born out of obedience to a holy calling.

●　　●　　●　　●

As Madeleine taught more and more aspiring writers, she began articulating a unique, transformative understanding of art as a spiritual discipline. "To serve a work of art is almost identical with adoring the Master of the Universe in contemplative prayer," she would often say.[10] For Madeleine, writing wasn't just a hobby to be done on the side while attending to other, more legitimate work. It was a God-given vocation that deserved the same attentiveness as prayer—indeed, that writing itself can be a form of worship that brings us into the presence of God.

Her students, she discovered, had never heard anything like this. The divide between sacred and secular had become so great that imaginative creativity was perceived—both by artists and people of faith—as something wholly at odds with religion. You were either a practicing artist or a practicing Christian, but you couldn't be both.

Luci Shaw was the one who convinced Madeleine, in the late 1970s, to compile her thoughts on faith and writing into a book. "About six or eight months later she had come to visit again," Luci told me, "and she handed me this typescript—we didn't have computers, it was all typewriters—she had this typescript of paper that was probably half an inch thick and it was really kind of messy. And she kind of threw it at me and said, 'Well here it is, do what you want with it. It has no shape.'" Over the next few weeks, Luci recalled, "I pulled the whole thing apart and made little piles on my living room floor of things, chapters and words that seemed to work together. And I put it back in a new ordering of the chapters and ideas, and handed it back to her, and she was thrilled." The shapeless mass, transformed by Luci, came out in 1980 as *Walking on Water: Reflections on Faith and Art.*

Robert Hudson, writer and longtime editor in Christian publishing, wrote, "*Walking on Water* shaped my life as a writer. I read it in the early 1980s while attending a somewhat restrictive church. I'd just had a broken engagement, was depressed, and was questioning the value of my writing altogether. *Walking on Water* (maybe even a little more than metaphorically) saved my life at a time when I was thinking pretty dark thoughts. I've read many of Madeleine's books, but that one is closest to my heart."

Novelist Leif Enger (*Peace Like a River*), in his foreword to the 2003 edition of Madeleine's *Penguins and Golden Calves*, tells of how he struggled in the 1980s to understand the role of faith in the writing life. "The few examples of sanctioned 'Christian fiction' I'd picked up," he wrote, "had been earnest, evangelical, and drafted to a set of closely drawn boundaries that sucked out all prospects for spontaneity and joy."[11] He was beginning to fear that any attempt to reconcile faith with the longing to write meant that "one of the two had to die." Leif was then given Madeleine's *Walking on Water*, in which she asserted things like, "We live by revelation, as Christians, as artists, which means that we must be careful never to get set into rigid molds."[12] Leif began to wonder, "Could God really be so generous? Might he actually want us to do those things we desire most? Could he—it seemed almost heretical—have *designed* us to want and to accomplish those things?"[13]

Walking on Water was a game-changer. And Enger wasn't the first, nor the last, writer to find in Madeleine a patron saint of the arts. Jeffrey Overstreet, who teaches film and creative writing at Seattle Pacific University, told me, "I can't count how many artists I've met who just light up when you mention that book. And they will talk to you about that as their passport into their life of faith and imagination, where there is harmony between vocabularies of faith and vocabularies of creative writing and craftsmanship and the dedication required to achieve excellence."

A key concept in the book is Madeleine's insistence on the role of the artist as a religious vocation: that artistic practices *are* religious practices, whether or not the artist is aware of it. And, conversely, religious practices, for the artist, are not somehow compartmentalized from the creative process but, rather, all of a piece. The artist, while creating, is in some kind of communion with the Maker who made us in his own image—who made us to make things—which has implications not only for individual artists but also for religious communities and their engagement with the arts.

Overstreet described growing up in an extremely conservative Baptist church: "I'm grateful for many things I learned there, but one of its weaknesses was an extreme suspicion of, fear of, and avoidance of the imagination." He said, "It was *Walking on Water*, during my senior year of high school, that changed my life probably more than any work of nonfiction outside of the Bible itself." Indeed, "So much of what L'Engle was writing about was trying to reclaim Christian freedom and the value of the imagination. . . . There are so many lines from that book that I know as thoroughly, and have taken to heart as deeply, as many of the Scriptures that have shaped my life."

Poet Marci Rae Johnson, a colleague from my Wheaton College days and editor for WordFarm, told me, "My senior year of high school I had decided that I not only wanted to read books but write them as well." As was the case with Jeffrey, "*Walking on Water* was full of the type of encouragement and advice I needed—not only as a writer, but as a Christian struggling to define my own beliefs after a fundamentalist upbringing as well as a Christian trying to see how and whether one could be both Christian and artist. And indeed, for Madeleine the two were tightly and irrevocably connected." (If we haven't learned by now that *Walking on Water* makes a great graduation gift, we're not paying attention.)

For Aleah Marsden, whose life has recently transformed from write-at-home-mom to seminary student, "Madeleine gave me permission to use my imagination in a way that feels holy. I had never considered that my fantasies and fascinations could be tools used to point people to truth in a way that they may never otherwise find it." The childhood creativity so often squashed in adulthood becomes, with Madeleine, something to be cultivated. Aleah told me, "She gave dignity to my daydreaming, that my art was actually a vital expression of the gifts I had been given and therefore a responsibility."

When I myself am not writing, I feel cut off from God, committing a sin of omission by failing to do what I was made for. As a Christian, I'm not only called to serve Jesus but I'm called to "serve the work" that Jesus gave me, as Madeleine put it—indeed, serving the work *is* to serve Jesus. "The artist is a servant who is willing to be a birth giver. In a very real sense the artist (male or female) should be like Mary, who, when the angel told her that she was to bear the Messiah, was obedient to the command."[14] Like Mary, we respond to our calling by saying, "I am the Lord's servant. May your word to me be fulfilled" (Luke 1:38).

Art is not merely a task but also a kind of spiritual surrender.

•   •   •   •

While there's no secret sauce to obedience—you literally sit down in a chair and start stringing nouns and verbs together— the artist still attends to excellence of the craft. "When we write a story, we must write to the absolute best of our ability," Madeleine said. "That is the job, first and foremost. If we are truly Christian, that will be evident, no matter what the topic. If we are not truly Christian, that will also be evident, no matter how pious the tale."[15] We don't throw things like active verbs, complex characters, or interesting plots out the window. This is how we love the Lord our God with all our heart, soul, strength *and* mind (see Luke 10:27), as so many writers of faith have done before us.

In *Walking on Water* Madeleine famously insists that we judge a book not by whether it deals with "Christian" topics or promotes our personal worldview, but whether it has merit as a work of art. None of that changes just because the publishing market or the target readership gives far too many books a pass in favor of some other social or political agenda.

My husband once unwittingly checked out a book from the library that had been among my pile of nos for that judging season. He made it a few chapters into what I knew was a historical Christian romance (I didn't let on), but then he flung it aside. When I asked why, he said, "I quit when the book said, 'He looked at her, not lustily, but with admiration.' And I thought, *Oh, hell, no.*" It wasn't because of its genre, nor that its author wasn't a trained historian, but because of its sanitized view of human relationships that delivers all the feel-good, wish-fulfillment stuff ("He loves me for my smarts!") but leaves out the mess, the brokenness—or even the good gifts of a body designed by God. This is an incomplete, if not willfully dishonest, portrait of the human condition. Which is bad art.

Madeleine would've been horrified, of course. "If it's bad art, it's bad religion, no matter how pious the subject." This is a strong statement, stronger than most of us are willing to make. Who are we to judge someone else's religion? And yet it's through the weaknesses of our art that the weaknesses of our theology are exposed.

I'm indebted to my theology professor J. Kameron Carter (*Race: A Theological Account*), who introduced his students to the metaphor of jazz improvisation as central to our theological task. Only once we've mastered a particular school or tradition (whether it's an artistic medium or theology) can we both improvise on it *and* critique its performance by others. Black Christians in America, for instance, haven't thrown out the Bible just because it's been used to defend the distorted racialized theology of white Christianity; rather, people of color have studied, sung, and performed the Scriptures such that those texts become a prophetic challenge to the tradition from the inside out. Like jazz performance, religious belief and practice are a kind of artistic training: repetition, memorization, daily reps are how you learn. Eventually you gain the freedom for creative play as well as your own prophetic voice.

Madeleine would've concurred. Very few of us are original

geniuses. But once we demonstrate mastery of the essentials, we are given tremendous freedom to improvise our unique contribution. Mrs Whatsit's metaphor of the sonnet comes to mind: "You mean you're comparing our lives to a sonnet? A strict form, but freedom within it?" Calvin asks her, and she replies, "Yes. You're given the form, but you have to write the sonnet yourself. What you say is completely up to you."[16] British author G. K. Chesterton once said of his conversion to Catholicism, "The more I considered Christianity, the more I found that while it had established a rule and order, the chief aim of that order was to give room for good things to run wild."[17] There is a pattern to faith that provides both boundaries and meaning; but within the structure we improvise. And this too is both an artistic and a spiritual discipline.

●　　●　　●　　●

For many artists of faith, the trick to integrating faith and art comes in not making artistic practice a *substitute* for religious practice. It's tempting, once we find our creative people, to make those the only spiritual family we have. I've known many a writer who, upon attending a writing conference for the first time, felt like a refugee among other refugees who speak his or her mother tongue: Oh, the relief of being understood! of realizing you're not the only one who thinks this way! If the writing life expresses the deepest longings of our souls—while church, on the other hand, sometimes feels like a foreign, even hostile, country—then it's easy to bail on communal worship altogether.

Lisa Ann Cockrel, who directs the Calvin College Festival of Faith and Writing, reflected with me on the tension between the arts and faith communities: "You're driven to make art out of questions, not answers," she said. "I think that writers, visual artists, musicians, they seek out communities where questions can be explored without fear and also a kind of joy. I don't know that our churches are those kinds of places." This is where Madeleine's influence has been so powerful for people like Lisa and her colleagues. "Madeleine did become, for my cohort in college—for my friends who were also kind of bookish and were interested in pop culture—an interesting enough figure that when my best friend from college moved to New York City on a Teach for America stint, she actually started attending All Angels' specifically because it was Madeleine L'Engle's church."

All Angels' is known, not incidentally, for giving primacy of place to the arts. But this is a rare example. It's the distressing unwillingness of many faith communities to allow for the possibility of God's grace in artistic practice that has contributed to those communities being hostile environments for artists. "It is nearly impossible be an artist today," painter Makoto Fujimura told me, "to be seen in the artist's full, authentic self. The church makes this even harder, I am afraid, trapped in limited-resource thinking and utilitarian pragmatism." We are perfectly happy to organize church golf outings, for instance, but we are far less willing to expend resources on the materials it takes for artists to pursue their crafts.

D. L. Mayfield lives and serves in a refugee neighborhood in Portland, Oregon, a missional vocation that often feels at odds with the writing life. "Madeleine makes me, an incredibly utilitarian activist, believe in the mumbo-jumbo language of creativity," she reflected with me; "of what it means when you don't just write down what is right, but you write down what is true. When I get lost in my world of trying to do the most good, it is people like Madeleine who call me to something bigger, something that will last much longer."

All of these conversations beg a number of questions: In what ways are we, as a Christian body, bracketing art into some other, less valuable category, something subpar to other vocations or ministries such as missions or preaching or running health clinics? In what ways are we diminishing the roles of the artists in our midst by framing their jobs as secular (and expensive) hobbies rather than as vital for the spiritual upbuilding of the whole community? By contrast, in Makoto's words, "L'Engle brought her language of creativity and imagination to the fore of our discussions, and thereby mediated the gap between the church and the world. Her language is the antidote to the modern malaise of scarcity mindset."

Things don't always go swimmingly once churches become tentatively open to the arts, however. Spoken word poet Amena Brown, in a podcast episode for *Christianity Today*, said, "What I've found sometimes in a faith-based setting is there's a way people want art to go. And they either want it to have answers and not have unanswered questions in it, or they want it to have faith and not doubt, or they want it to be so spiritual that it is no longer human."[18] Artists continually find themselves playing the role of apologist to their fellow believers—a role that can become exhausting over time. And yet, if Madeleine taught us nothing else, she taught us a kind of tenacious compassion for those to whom we've been called.

Overstreet told me, "She shows imaginative believers how to speak the truth back to the church, but to speak the truth in love." Madeleine the apologist at times became Madeleine the prophet: "You can tell she's frustrated with the church, you can tell she's angry. But she never separates herself from the church and points a finger. She stands within the church and insists on what the gospel gives us, insists on the full vision, saying, 'Don't deprive me of the riches of Christ's teaching.'" For Jeffrey, "That was an incredible model for me. I hear so many voices like that now that have to trace those sentiments back to her."

Like Madeleine, we face a choice to live out our faith on the ground, with real people in all their messiness, because this is part of our artistic obedience. We not only have something to say as writers, but our fellow believers need to hear it.

●   ●   ●   ●

"If it's good art . . . ," Madeleine says, leaving us hanging by those ellipses; "and there the questions start coming, questions which it would be simpler to evade."[19] She goes on to assert that God is no respecter of persons or religious beliefs when it comes to giftedness, that indeed, the Holy Spirit uses all kinds of otherwise "secular" or even "non-Christian" things to touch us on a spiritual level, whether or not the artist intended it.

Given the nature of the CT awards, I'm not generally facing the question of how to judge art by non-Christian authors. But the experience has given me a particular lens by which to view all literature. I'm often asked if it's really possible to gauge a good book just by the opening sentences, for instance. As any literary agent or editor will tell you, the answer is yes. Give us a snippet of dialogue, a paragraph of description, a brief glimpse of the author's worldview, and we'll know. Editors read so many proposals (remember: they do this every day, all year long) that they're pretty good at spotting what doesn't work. What's harder is finding the book that *does*.

Some of what shapes the criteria is the publishing house's brand, its unique mission and vision, its own target readership or tribe. These factors set pretty clear limitations on what can be considered, regardless of the editor's own personal literary tastes. The same is true for my role as a preliminary fiction judge. CT's mission is "equipping Christians to renew their minds, serve the church, and create culture to the glory of God"—so my job isn't to decide which books are my personal favorites (often, after judging, I'll go back and indulge in a few on my own). Rather, my job is to ascertain what books best reflect CT's mission, particularly the third item, *creating culture*. I'm not looking for authors who merely reflect the already-cherished values and attitudes of a Christian subculture; rather, I'm looking for writers who generate art that intentionally seeks to *engage, transform,* and *contribute* to culture at large.

In short, my modest task as fiction judge is to discern which books have the best chance of still being on the shelves—of Christians and non-Christians alike—in a hundred years.

What authors of Christian faith will have their obituaries written up, as Madeleine did, by the *New York Times*? Whose fiftieth-anniversary editions will send their publishers into a frenzy of celebration, as Macmillan did for *Wrinkle* in 2012? Whose novel, when translated into a blockbuster film depicting the main characters as a multiracial family (as in director Ava DuVernay's recent version of *Wrinkle*), will inspire an entire demographic that may have never read the story before? This isn't to say a work only has merit if the author gains the attention of mainstream media or if the book earns key placement in trade bookstores or is published by a trade (rather than Christian) publishing house. Rather, as Madeleine said, "If the artist reflects only his own culture, then his works will die with that culture. But if his works reflect the eternal and universal, they will revive."[20]

Ultimately, the task for any novelist of faith is not to shore up the cherished values of a tribe that believes itself to be under siege. It's first to worship the living God, to love him with everything you've got: heart, mind, soul, and strength. And the second task of the artist of faith is wrapped up in Christ's own commission to his disciples in Matthew 28:19–20: "Therefore *go* and make disciples of all nations" [emphasis added]. This is not the same as a "misguided attempt to protect the truth *from* culture," as Overstreet said to me, but "to bring the truth *to* culture."

So, we make good art, and we hope that by doing so we have offered up an honest, well-executed gift of worship to the Maker who designed us to make things. And we share that work with our fellow readers—not just our fellow believers, but all story-loving humans—because not only do we want them to experience our own delight in making it, but also because, as people of faith, we are called to play a small part in transforming the culture in which we live. Our works become icons: windows by which others can see the "light so lovely." And by this, we hope, lives can be changed. Including our own.

"Writing fiction, then, for L'Engle, is not merely a way of ordering life," wrote scholar Don Hettinga, "it is a way of living it. The choices before a storyteller as she composes are the same spiritual and moral decisions that any individual confronts daily. The effect that a writer has then also bears moral consequences."[21] For Madeleine, those effects were overwhelmingly positive in the lives of thousands of students and readers. But now we must make the turn toward a more difficult chapter, in which we also acknowledge that not all of her artistic decisions—particularly her propensity to blur fact and fiction—let in the light.

Chapter Six

FACT *and* FICTION

We have to be braver than we think we can be, because
God is constantly calling us to be more than we are, to
see through plastic sham to living, breathing reality,
and to break down our defenses of self-protection in
order to be free to receive and give love.

Walking on Water

When I was a child, my family lived for several years in
an economically depressed area of rural upstate New
York. Our 110-year-old parsonage sat next door to my father's
Presbyterian church, built in 1825 after the spiritual revival of
the Second Great Awakening. Next door, a graveyard with tilting headstones dated back to the late 1700s; and beyond those,
farm fields stretched in all directions. There in the region that
revivalist Charles Finney had called the "burned-over district,"
where the fires of the Holy Spirit once swept the landscape, a
small cluster of houses and barns along the state road was all
that remained of our hamlet.

One Saturday evening, we had gone a mile down the road for dinner at a parishioner's home when the sirens started. First one firetruck blared past, then another. Then more, wailing in the dark. And they didn't pass out of hearing but instead remained at some fixed point in the near distance.

Eventually my father rose and went to the window. Above the treetops, roughly where our hamlet stood, the sky glowed orange.

"I need to go," he said. "That could be the church. Or the house."

He was out the door within seconds, accompanied by our host. I recall a tense quarter of an hour while the children stirred restlessly, the women speculating in quiet tones so as not to alarm us. Then the phone rang. It was my father from the parsonage. A nearby barn blazed violently. So far, the church and the parsonage were safe, but firemen were everywhere: on our rooftops, in the fields, hosing down the church, stamping out sparks and small blazes all over the property. We were to stay put until things were under control.

It was a long night, I remember. The barn was a total loss. Eventually we were allowed to come home for bed, but firemen remained long after, monitoring the blaze. Sunday morning dawned with gray smoke and ash rising from the ruins next door; and while we thanked God during worship that our historic buildings were saved, I'll never forget standing at a window during coffee hour watching a wraithlike coil of smoke drift up lazily from the hollow of an ancient stump behind the church. Even after the fire had burned itself out, it smoked for days, an eerie reminder that as much as we might desire a nice, tidy resolution to a crisis, such an ending is not, ultimately, guaranteed.

If this story sounds familiar to Madeleine L'Engle fans, it's because she tells a similar tale in the first of her autobiographical Crosswicks Journals, *A Circle of Quiet*. Hers is much more eloquent, of course, with a wonderful setup about an unpopular new family, the Brechsteins, who alienated everyone in the Franklins' small town; and the heroism of a certain grumpy farmer who saves the Brechsteins' children when their house catches fire. You can imagine how riveted I was the first time I read it: Gosh, but that same thing happened to me! Our hamlet too had its grumpy farmer. My parents, the newcomers, were considered outsiders too; we never felt entirely at home. Sure, not all of Madeleine's details lined up with mine: it wasn't our house that burned; my sister and I didn't need saving. And our story didn't have a feel-good ending either—if anything, my parents were treated unkindly as the years went by. But I'd experienced a similar small-town scenario. Madeleine got it right.

Even more striking, her version had such an "all shall be well" tone, as if, deep down, no matter our petty differences, real people can come together in a crisis, overlook our troubles, and make the world a better place. Her version had everything I'd wished had been resolved in our own family's story, in that strange and unhappy corner of the Finger Lakes that we left, a few years later, without ever desiring to return. Her story is what I wanted my own to be.

Except, in Madeleine's case, it never happened.

● ● ● ●

"My husband says, and I'm afraid with justification," Madeleine wrote in *A Circle of Quiet*, "that by the time I've finished a book

I have no idea what in it is fabrication and what is actuality; and he adds that this holds true not only for novels but for most of my life. We do live, all of us, on many different levels, and for most artists the world of imagination is more real than the world of the kitchen sink."[1] There were no Brechsteins, she went on to explain—or at least no family with that surname and those exact circumstances. There was no grumpy farmer—or rather, there were lots of grumpy farmers all rolled into one person. Fires came and went in that small town, and heroics indeed happened. But the main thing, the significant point for Madeleine, was that "the emotional premise of the sketch, the feeling of being a stranger and sojourner—all of this is true. This is the way it is."[2]

Stories are about what *happens*, Madeleine insisted, not just about what *happened*. As a writer myself, I know this, of course. If I can't express my themes universally, then I have only succeeded in reporting disjointed events, not narrating a deeper truth. And yet my reaction to having been emotionally invested in a purportedly nonfiction work, only to discover the episode wasn't factual, gives me pause. What else in her "nonfiction" have I been assuming was biographically accurate? What about the ways I narrate my own life? And what do our loved ones think of all this?

The Brechstein story is an example of Madeleine's insistence on truth taking primacy over facts. This is a key trope in both her fiction and her nonfiction. As her housemate Barbara Braver told me, just because you know the fact that water boils at a certain temperature doesn't mean you know what water really *is*, what it symbolizes, what truth it holds. The same can be said of the human life. I can prove all sorts of facts about you scientifically, but this in no way sums up your ontological worth, your purpose, your dignity as a human being made in the image of God.

"Thinking about the Brechsteins," Madeleine mused, "attempting the not-quite possible task of separating fact from fiction in this sketch, teaches me something about the nature of reality. On one level, one might say that the Brechsteins are not real. But they are. It is through the Brechsteins, through the world of the imagination which takes us beyond the restrictions of provable fact, that we touch the hem of truth."[3]

The phrase "beyond provable fact" surfaces over and over in Madeleine's fiction and nonfiction, and it's not merely a literary assertion about the nature of story: for Madeleine it's a key theological point. "We do not need faith for facts; we do need faith for truth."[4] If I have all the facts about God, I don't need faith to believe in him, do I? Certainly, as we already explored in chapter four, we continue to learn new facts about the universe every single day. But this doesn't change the essential nature of God, whose character isn't bound by what we can or can't prove.

"How do I happen to believe in God?" wrote Frederick Buechner in *The Alphabet of Grace*; "Writing novels, I got into the habit of looking for plots. After a while, I began to suspect that my own life had a plot. And after a while more, I began to suspect that life itself has a plot." It's human nature to descry patterns and meaning in our daily experience, to attempt to narrate events such that they fit our preferred way of scripting the world. Yet, if our lives veer off script while we're living them—if crises strike, if people say and do things that don't fit the storyline—we tend toward one of two responses: denial, which takes many forms, or existential despair, which also takes many forms.

Sometimes denial and despair are bound up together in

one person (there's *both/and* again), or even in one emotional outburst. There's no guarantee we'll be honest, clever, or heroic in the critical moment. But for the inveterate storytellers among us, myself included, the impulse toward denial often manifests as a creative manhandling of the facts in order to tell the story we want our lives to be.

My tale of the fire is true. It's a story of what happens in our human experience: crises, fear, heroism, loss, change. It's also factual: not only was I there to witness these events as they happened, but I also ran the beginning of this chapter past my parents to confirm that what I remembered was, in fact, accurate. (It was my father who pointed out the revivalist history of that region, including Charles Finney's description of it as the "burned-out district.") Accountability has been my practice throughout my writing career: "Does this sound right to you?" I ask family and friends, handing them a couple of pages from a manuscript. "Is this how you remember it?" It's my way of not merely relying on my own sketchy memories, which have been known to fail spectacularly ("I've no idea what you're talking about," my husband often says of a memory I assume we share). Instead I try to acknowledge that my version of events doesn't hold more authority just because I wrote it down.

While I desire to tell stories of what *happens*, I'm also obligated—by the sheer material reality of being a fallible mortal among other fallible mortals, bound to others for daily survival—to keep myself accountable to what *happened*. Because if God can work through fiction, as Madeleine insisted, we must also assert that God can, and does, work through facts.

● ● ● ●

If God created this material world, then God created facts. I may not like them: I will crash if I attempt to defy gravity by jumping off my roof; I will burn my hand if I touch a flame. Indeed, my material body proves the facts of physics all day long, for better or worse. This may not be the sum total of my existence, but I can't ignore that matter *matters*. After all, as Madeleine herself would be the first to remind us, God made matter and called it good.

Meanwhile, there are certain historical claims I cling to as a Christian, without which my faith would be meaningless. Jesus was a real, live person. His disciples actually touched his resurrected body. He didn't dismiss his disciple Thomas for refusing to believe without proof (see John 20:24–29). Rather, Jesus gave Thomas the means for proving it ("Touch my scars . . . here and here . . .") and then later cooked and ate fish in the disciples' presence, for good measure.

"I stand with Paul here," Madeleine wrote of the apostle's claims about the resurrection in 1 Corinthians 15:12–19. "When we deny the Resurrection, we are denying Christianity. We are no longer the Church; no wonder the secular world is horrified by us." Paul himself wrote, "If Christ has not been raised, your faith is futile; you are still in your sins. Then those also who have fallen asleep in Christ are lost. If only for this life we have hope in Christ, we are of all people most to be pitied" (1 Corinthians 15:17–19). The gospel isn't just a "good spell," an enchanting story; it's also good news.

Facts matter. Yet Madeleine's insistence on truth taking primacy over facts is one of those rare instances when a woman who otherwise excelled at being *both/and* tended toward *either/or*. At times she wandered into a false binary—you can have truth *or* facts but not both—as if facts themselves can't carry truth. She never comes out and says so: but in positioning stories as the primary vehicles for truth, the assumption is that facts are only secondary, and suspect.

She rightly challenged our tendency to assume that correlation means causation: just because something is told in the form of a narrative doesn't mean it never happened, nor even that it lies. The biblical book of Job may have been written as a kind of ancient Near Eastern opera, but its literary form doesn't automatically mean that a character like Job never existed—no more than the artistic form of a musical somehow suggests that composer Lin-Manuel Miranda invented politician Alexander Hamilton. Yet Madeleine never really reckoned with the converse: just because you tell something in the form of narrative does not mean it automatically delivers truth.

The story may be true for you, the author; but what if it contradicts someone else's truth? What if, in contradicting someone else's truth, you end up hurting or even silencing them?

● ● ● ●

My first hint that I was sailing into difficult waters, as a biographer, was in coming across the 2004 *New Yorker* profile, "The Storyteller: Fact, Fiction, and the Books of Madeleine L'Engle" by Cynthia Zarin. I've already mentioned Zarin's interviews with the family, whose responses to Madeleine's work were, in Madeleine's own words, "ambivalent."[5] I immediately wondered what the family thought of the article: Was it fair reporting? How much could be chalked up to editorial manhandling? (A lot, apparently.)

Then, reading Leonard Marcus's interviews with Madeleine's contemporaries in *Listening for Madeleine* only complexified an already complex picture. In one example, author and family friend Katharine Weber told Marcus, "*Two-Part Invention* is a beautiful portrait of the marriage she wished she had."[6] Madeleine's former son-in-law, Alan Jones, likewise said, "While I don't think her marriage was at all disastrous, it was complicated, and *Two-Part Invention* was a tremendously idealized picture of the marriage. I always thought the title was suitably ironical."[7]

Madeleine's eldest daughter, Josephine, recalled instances in which Madeleine's fans would approach the family, exclaiming how they felt like they knew the family so well. Josephine told Marcus, "I would always reply, 'You have to remember that my mother is a fiction writer.' 'No, no,' they would say as if I had somehow misunderstood them. 'I'm talking about her nonfiction.'" And so Josephine would repeat, with as much patience as she could muster, "You have to remember that she is a fiction writer."[8] I'm struck by how much hurt and love and bewilderment and courage is bound up in such an exchange.

Pause. This is one of those moments when the ground you thought was stable starts tremoring—particularly when you're a biographer attempting to paint a faithful portrait of a life. If it weren't for the gracious input of Madeleine's granddaughter Charlotte, who is Josephine and Alan's youngest daughter and literary executor of the L'Engle estate, I might still be sitting amidst a heap of books, wailing, "Help!"

Charlotte's take on her grandmother's storytelling is powerfully charitable. She explains that it's not that Madeleine was lying. Rather, Madeleine was, like every good storyteller, *embellishing.* The point of a given story might be true—such as, manuscripts get rejected a lot—and along the way Madeleine supplied the concrete details every good writing teacher asks for: so, for instance, *A Wrinkle in Time* was rejected twenty-seven times. Or thirty. Or thirty-seven. (By the 2003 anthology *Winning Authors: Profiles of the Newbery Medalists,* compiled by Kathleen Long Bostrom from author interviews, the number had risen to "over forty."[9]) I can picture Madeleine shrugging. Details, details. The point is, authors can plan on their manuscripts getting rejected. A lot. That's *true.*

Despite her resistance to provable facts, however, Madeleine would nevertheless insist, to the exasperation of her family, that her own recall of particular events was accurate. Charlotte told me that for all her grandmother's emphasis on embracing uncertainty, Madeleine *did* want answers; and once she found or created ones that satisfied her, she would insist on them as the only possible interpretation of events her family may have remembered very differently. "On the empirical level," Madeleine wrote in *A Circle of Quiet,* "if we have a family argument about when or where something happened, and the others don't agree with me, if I say, 'But I know I'm right this time, I'll go get my journal,' they usually give up"[10]—as if a personal journal presents incontrovertible evidence rather than a potentially fallible interpretation.

For those closest to Madeleine, despite their deep love for her and vice versa, this sort of episode was not an isolated incident; it felt like a regular erasure of their experience. Alan Jones reflected with Leonard Marcus, "I think it was very hard on her children when they'd say something about a personal experience and she'd say, 'No. It didn't happen that way. I have it in my journal.' That was a way of somehow denying other people's experience."[11] It didn't seem to matter that her loved ones had a different version of events. "Madeleine was such a good writer," Jones said, "and she would work things out in her journal and idealize reality, and I think she sometimes thought of it as objective truth. We all do that to some extent, inventing our lives as we go along. Madeleine was a storyteller looking for a story."

Madeleine's fiction, meanwhile, often hit far too close to home. In *Meet the Austins*, for example, the family welcomes a troubled orphan, Maggy, into their midst, which sets off a chain of events that threaten to tear the otherwise mostly perfect family apart. The book came out in 1960, a mere four years after the Franklins too had adopted an orphan, Maria. "How could she have done that?" Maria's friends would ask her, according to Zarin's article. Maria asserted, not surprisingly, "I hated the Austin books."[12]

Madeleine, for her part, claimed that Maggy bore no resemblance to Maria—that her characters rose unbidden from some other place entirely. "Reality," Madeleine wrote in *A Circle of Quiet*: "I can only affirm that the people in my stories have as complete and free a life of their own as do my family and friends."[13] The only exceptions to not knowing where her characters sprang from, she claimed, were Canon Tallis, who was based on her friend Canon West, and "Rob Austin, who simply is our youngest child [Bion], and there's nothing I can do about it."[14]

Rob Austin is protagonist Vicky's little brother, memorable for his delightful sayings. In *Meet the Austins* Rob prays, "Oh, and God bless Santa Claus, and bless you, too, God"[15]—taken, most likely, from things Bion Franklin actually said. Eerily, as Cynthia Zarin points out in her *New Yorker* article, Rob never seems to grow up from book to book: he's always the baby of the family, acting and speaking like a five-year-old, even as his older siblings age into early adulthood. If Rob wasn't granted the freedom to grow and change, what of Bion himself? What happens to a child who finds himself—his real, not fictionalized self—written into novels by his own mother as the eternal preschooler?

According to Madeleine in *Walking on Water*, at ten years old Bion became upset with her for (spoiler alert) killing off the character Joshua in drafts she read aloud from *The Arm of the Starfish*.[16] Bion demanded that she change it. She insisted that she couldn't—because, in her words, "that's what happened." The two went back and forth, but Madeleine held her ground. Joshua's death remained. And according to Madeleine, Bion wouldn't read anything else of hers for years. However, her various editors described the massive revisions she would undergo—sometimes at their suggestions, other times just because she could—down to major plot changes that the editors didn't even feel were necessary. So, on some levels, yes, she *could* change it.

When who you are is so heavily scripted by someone else, the lines between fiction and fact must seem very blurred indeed. Who is the person acting and speaking here, me or the person my parent invented? Can I change the narrative of my own story if I want to? As Charlotte says in *Listening for Madeleine*, "How do you live up to that legacy? How do you make yourself real to your own mother?"[17] When Bion died of liver failure from alcoholism at age forty-seven, the rest of the family spoke openly about it—which, as Charlotte told me, was a way to break the cultural silence around alcoholism and make room for others who might be going through a similar experience. Yet Madeleine refused to acknowledge it.

We are, none of us, discrete authorial units. We live and write in community; our account of events is put in conversation with other accounts, and this is what we call accountability. When it comes to the impact of Madeleine's storytelling on her family, hers might be a cautionary tale. To what extent are we leveraging our own preferred plotlines at the expense of giving our loved ones as "complete and free a life of their own" as we hope to give our invented characters, even our invented selves?

●　●　●　●

When I asked Madeleine's housemate, Barbara Braver, about Madeleine's spin on real events, she reflected, "When you look at the fact of the situation, it may not speak to the deeper reality. That's what storytelling is all about. In the telling of the story it's not that you're making things up; it's that you're touching on the ineffable, you're touching on the things that are too complicated to name in rational terms. That's what storytellers do. They tell stories in ways that you understand the deeper truth beyond the fact. That's one thing Madeleine had a huge gift for." Elsewhere, in *Listening for Madeleine*, Barbara told Marcus, "Something might be factually correct but still lead you to the wrong conclusion."[18] "Indeed it might," countered Cara Parks in a *New Republic* review of Marcus's book, "but our current age has no patience for useful fictions presenting themselves as fact."[19]

We now live—in a phrase that would astound and possibly confound L'Engle—in a "post-truth" and "alternative facts" culture. Sifting the real from fake news is a skillset some of us have only recently recognized as urgent. Facts are not only hotly contested in favor of various ideological fictions, but the fictions can be alarmingly persuasive and even harmful to real people on the ground. As a result, we've learned to approach everything with what my theology professor, J. Kameron Carter, called a "hermeneutics of suspicion"—something that communities of color have employed for centuries. Whom does this interpretation of events benefit? Why? What other voices also need amplifying?

If Madeleine tended to script individuals, she also had a tendency to script demographic groups. According to Madeleine, children are *always* open to mystery. (Really? My eldest son takes comfort in predictability, actually.) Teens, meanwhile, "love the combination of order and delight in a Bach fugue."[20] (Do they? Let's test that theory at my church's teen ministry on Sunday nights.) Adults are *always* doing something boneheaded and unimaginative—are we? Native Americans were peaceful and earth loving before the European invasion—were they? Questions turn to discomfort when I read about the supposedly salvific role of indigenous characters with fair hair or blue eyes, descendants of European ancestors, in books like *Dragons in the Waters* and *A Swiftly Tilting Planet*.

To some extent, like many of her fellow mainline liberals, Madeleine succumbed to what C. S. Lewis called the "myth of progress." She wrote in *Walking on Water* in 1980, "It is hard for us to believe now that there were anti-vaccinationists, when vaccinations have succeeded in wiping smallpox from the planet"[21]—as if that was ancient history never to be repeated.

Her tendency toward obliviousness about the recurring

history of racism and classism also crops up in various places, although she was at least culturally aware enough to notice the problems in a story like Frances Hodgson Burnett's *The Little Princess*. In her introduction to the 1987 Bantam Books edition of that classic, she admits that

> when I [as a child] was reading and rereading Sara's adventures, England was still an empire, and it had not occurred to many of us that empires are made by taking other peoples' lands, by imposing our culture on ones quite different from ours, with a bland assumption that of course our culture is the best one and that these "primitive" peoples are savages and are really lucky to have their land and their gods and their uncouth customs taken away.[22]

And yet, she says that later, as a young woman, when she began to notice those problems with Burnett's story, "I was inchoately grateful that in my country we believe that all men and women are created equal." She never offers a corrective to this starry-eyed view of American ideals, although she acknowledges, "In our own country, which I think is as free from caste as any country on this planet, [the problem of inherent privilege] still exists, and calling a garbage collector a sanitation engineer simply emphasizes it."[23]

Madeleine's occasional tone deafness to the complex layers of race and class, to what black feminists now refer to as "intersectionality," we're tempted to look back on as generational. A longtime friend of the Franklins' children, Gretchen Gubelman—who stayed with the family in Manhattan as a young woman in 1964—told Marcus in *Listening for Madeleine*, "I was also deeply involved in the civil rights movement, Vietnam War protests, the Student Nonviolent Coordinating Committee, and SDS, and Hugh and Madeleine were more conservative politically than I was." She then described a cross-generational scene that still unfolds in our own era, every evening, in homes all across America: "When we argued and debated at dinnertime, it would feel as if we were starting from two completely different sets of facts."[24]

Lack of involvement in things like the civil rights movement, Madeleine herself insisted, were reasoned and intentional. She recalled praying to God about marching, and he told her she could reach more people with the pen. I'm not sure I'm satisfied with that answer, to be honest. In the mid-1960s she was a rising literary star. She still had teenagers in the house. One can understand if she didn't want to sabotage her career or disrupt her family. But who am I to question what God told her? Who are any of us? And that's the problem. How much do we script even God himself by fitting him into our personal narratives—or claim he has endorsed our version—of who we claim to be, rather than let God disrupt our stories with, for lack of a better word, facts?

If Madeleine was ever outspoken about injustice, it was about literary censorship—the effects of which she experienced firsthand and which she battled directly through advocating for authors as a member and one-time president of the Author's Guild. The inveterate storyteller was not particularly happy when censors wrested her own character away and scripted her as they wanted, depicting her as secretly New Age, for instance, a dangerous author trying to deceive Christian children.

It was her own Christian colleagues who helped her occasionally laugh about being mischaracterized and maligned. In the Chrysostom Society's rollicking serial murder mystery *Carnage at Christhaven*, Madeleine's fictionalized persona, Philippa d'Esprit, claims that her arch enemy, Ms. Emma Syss (nemesis, get it?), is somehow on the grounds of the Colorado resort where murders are taking place. Could Ms. Syss be the murderer? Another character, Stevens, isn't so sure. "It suddenly struck Stevens," wrote Calvin Miller in his assigned chapter, "that Philippa was the only one who had seen [Ms. Syss], and there was some doubt in his mind that Philippa could be trusted. She had once won an important literary medal in England, it was true, but it was also true that the book was a fantasy novel." Of all novelists, Stevens muses, "fantasy novelists were the last to be taken seriously."[25] The joke, of course, is that Stevens is based on real-life fantasy author, Stephen Lawhead, another member of the Society and contributor to the book. But underneath is a subtle critique of those writers who play fast and loose with the facts.

Madeleine's own tendencies, we might say, coming back to haunt her.

●   ●   ●   ●

For as long I've known him personally, Philip Yancey has been writing his own memoir. "It feels like fiction although it's based in fact," he told me. "I'm trying to make it as true as possible, but of course the techniques of memoir are more the techniques of fiction, things like dialogue and scene. But I'm quite aware that no memoir ever gets it right. We distort by selection;

we distort by our point of view. There's nothing more boring than a moment-by-moment account of what happened in my day, in my life." What he gleaned from Madeleine, he said, "was that she held firm to her core of beliefs and yet expressed an attitude of grace and inclusivity and a true humility that we're human beings, we don't always get it right. We never get it *all* right."

Fiction itself can be a distillation of the ways we sometimes get it wrong. Years ago, he says, while taking a course in fiction, he was working on a short story in which he tried not to fall into the usual writerly problems, such as creating two-dimensional characters who speak in clichés. "It was my world, and I was trying to make it true and authentic and compelling," he told me. "And then I got on the city bus and everyone spoke in clichés. There were no three-dimensional characters: they were all two-dimensional characters. They were stereotypes. That's the odd part of writing, you create this universe that only you inhabit, but you have to artificially create it in such a way that it sounds real even though clearly it's not real. And a great writer is able to do that."

But memoir is, in a sense, real. When I asked him whether he will get permission from existing people who appear in his memoir, he replied, "In some cases yes, and in some cases I would determine them to be unreliable sources. So I just have to make my own judgment. Some of the key characters are trustworthy, in my opinion. I don't make any promises that 'I'll change whatever you say.' It's only fair to make it known that they will be exposed, as it were. I've found it easier to deal with reactions before something reaches print than afterwards."

His favorite example comes from the story of Frank McCourt,

who wrote *Angela's Ashes*—which, Philip said, "is a wonderful memoir, very well constructed." According to Philip, "a journalist asked Frank's brother, 'Did you read Frank's book before it was published?' 'Nope,' the brother replied. 'Well, what did you think?' And the brother said 'I disagree with a lot of it. I remember it differently.' So the journalist went to Frank McCourt and said 'I talked to your brother and he said it didn't really happen that way.' And Frank said, 'Well, he should write his own damn memoir.' And the brother did."

When I shared that story to a roomful of Madeleine fans at the 2018 Festival of Faith and Writing, Charlotte and her sister Léna commented, "And that's the right answer." It doesn't matter how powerful an idol you might be, your writerly task, however difficult, is to make room for more voices than just your own.

Author and blogger Sarah Bessey told me that when she read Cynthia Zarin's *New Yorker* profile of Madeleine, it had a profound impact on how Sarah writes about her own family. "Back when I first started writing I wrote a lot about my children," she told me, "especially my older two, who are now fully functioning human beings with their own ideas. They've turned into these wonderful amazing people." But then she read the article, "and I remember having the realization that I was almost imposing a narrative on their life. It deeply changed how I wrote about my children, our community, our family's story."

For Sarah, the biggest concern "is exactly what Charlotte said: How do you make yourself real to someone who's fictionalized or created a narrative for who you are? That idea really haunts me as a mother because I think there's a lot of ways that parents do that to their children—whether parents are writers or not. How do you make sure you're actually seeing your children and knowing them and hearing them instead of, 'Well, here's how you were when you were two, and so I'll never let you break out of that mold'?" As Charlotte pointed out to me, when the parent is a writer it's even *more* difficult for the parent to allow the narrative to be challenged—because the story, on paper, is now bound up in the parent's public identity.

Several years ago Sarah wrote a blog post in which she included a conversation she'd had with one of her children about body image. The post went viral. But then, she recalls, "I felt so gross about it. Especially as the comments began pouring in of everybody diagnosing my child and giving me things to say or do. And I thought, 'Wait a minute, wait a minute, wait a minute: now people know this about my children.' I was mortified. I ended up having to delete that." In fact, Sarah told me, "I deleted a lot of stuff that I've written about my kids on my blog because I've realized I really misstepped. At some point I'm sure this new generation will begin to Google their parents. There will be moments when we'll have to say, 'You know what? I screwed up there. I shouldn't have said it. I shouldn't have done it. I fixed it later, but I shouldn't have done that. And I'm sorry.'"

For Sarah, "My children need to know that they're not copy to me. They need to know that their spiritual questions or moments or lives are not here for anyone else's consumption." But she also recognizes that this is hard for a lot of writers, "especially when parenting is a huge aspect of your life—a huge aspect of your own spirituality and awakening and how you understand God, how you're moving through the world." As with many women writers, "Faith is deeply connected to mothering for me. And how do I write about the ways mother-hood has been transformative, how it's become this crucible, without turning my children themselves into content?" And yet, Sarah cautions, none of us gets a pass just because we have some kind of unique calling. Not politicians, not pastors, not writers. "I refuse to believe I'm special."

When Sarah is out traveling and speaking, she continually meets people "who literally feel like they know me. They feel like we would be best friends in real life. They feel like they know my marriage and my children and my family. But you know what? They know the version I wrote. It's true as far as I'm concerned. Is it the whole truth? Nope. Is it the whole thing? Not at all. They'll be disappointed in me. I'm disgust-ingly normal. But there can be no pedestals here.

"The place where I have grief around Madeleine is that there's still this idea that she didn't do anything wrong. That other people were too sensitive. That they needed to get over it because it was in service of the almighty art, of the almighty story, of the almighty thing that was being created. But I don't think that anything we create trumps the people whom we love and who love us. We don't get to stomp all over their humanity in service of some mythic humanity. Learning how to hold that tension will be the work of a lifetime."

In the end, Sarah says, "No matter how much goodness and grace and richness someone like Madeleine has brought to our lives, acting like anyone is infallible—as if you shouldn't be able to look at their lives and say, 'I would do that dif-ferently,' or 'that's a blind spot or a tragedy'—diminishes the power of their work. You need to let them be a complicated human being."

• • • •

Madeleine's purportedly autobiographical events may or may not have happened, but to her, they were things that *happen*: they faithfully express the human experience; they point to the nature of God. And yet one gets the sense that she was aware, in some deep part of her spirit, that to play fast and loose with the facts at times diminished, rather than honored, those she loved. In one of her many sonnets—a poetic form that Luci Shaw says came to Madeleine effortlessly—Madeleine wrote to her husband Hugh in "To a Long Loved Love: 7":

> *Because you're not what I would have you be*
> *I blind myself to who, in truth, you are.*
> *Seeking mirage where desert blooms, I mar*
> *Your you. Aaah, I would like to see*
> *Past all delusion to reality:*
> *Then would I see God's image in your face,*
> *His hand in yours, and in your eyes his grace.*
> *Because I'm not what I would have me be,*
> *I idolize Two who are not any place,*
> *Not you, not me, and so we never touch.*
> *Reality would burn. I do not like it much.*
> *And yet in you, in me, I find a trace*
> *Of love which struggles to break through*
> *The hidden lovely truth of me, of you.*[*]

---

* "To a Long Loved Love: 7" from *The Weather of the Heart* by Madeleine L'Engle, copyright 1978 by Crosswicks, Ltd. Used by permission of WaterBrook Multnomah, an imprint of the Crown Publishing Group, a division of Penguin Random House LLC. All rights reserved. Any third party use of this material,

Part of our human brokenness is that we never fully know another person, not even our long-loved loves. And neither are we ever fully known. Only God, the one who made us, knows us in full—even better than we know ourselves. This is both a comfort and a struggle. But what I see in Madeleine, in this poetic moment, is the spiritual discipline of humility in the face of divine mystery, yet another Christian practice that we can lean into. We can take to heart this beautiful prayer by the first-century bishop Saint Clement of Rome, which Madeleine quotes in the afterword to Duane W. H. Arnold and Robert Hudson's book *Beyond Belief: What the Martyrs Said to God*:

> Almighty God, Father of our Lord Jesus Christ, grant, we pray, that we might be grounded and settled in your truth by the coming of your Holy Spirit into our hearts. What we do not know, reveal to us; what is lacking within us, make complete; that which we do know, confirm in us; and keep us blameless in your service, through Jesus Christ our Lord.[26]

Grant that we might be grounded and settled in your truth. Not our truth. Not the truth we wish for other people. God's truth.

In the end, we don't get to script others, much less ourselves. God is the author, not we humans, of our ongoing story—as the writer of Hebrews says, Jesus is "the author and finisher of our faith" (12:2 KJV). And just as God is the giver of truth via narrative, we can also hope, and pray, that God is the giver of truth via facts. Via events that really happen, to real people; not merely to events as we wish they would happen and to people as we wish them to be.

As much as Madeleine's family loves their matriarch, Charlotte told me, their choice to speak honestly is a way for them to grant Madeleine "the dignity of being human." When we make an idol of someone, we elevate them to an impossible plane. But when we treat someone with human dignity, with humility and grace, we allow her the chance to be, once again, an icon. Not an object to adore or shun but, rather, a window— rippled with imperfections, at times distorting our vision, but through which God's light can shine nonetheless.

At some point, however, the light will fade. Night will fall. Outside the window comes a growing, bewildering dusk. It's to those moments in Madeleine's story—and in our own lives— that we now turn.

Chapter Seven

LIGHT IN THE DARKNESS

"And we're not alone, you know, children," came
Mrs Whatsit, the comforter. "All through the universe it's being fought, all through the cosmos,
and my, but it's a grand and exciting battle."
A Wrinkle in Time

A few months shy of her seventy-third birthday in 1991, while being driven to a speaking gig in Escondido, California, Madeleine was chatting in the car with her hostess when a truck ran a red light and broadsided them. As Madeleine recounts in *The Rock That Is Higher*, while her hostess was obviously injured, Madeleine herself seemed, at first, merely sore. But at the hospital it became clear she had extensive internal damage and would require immediate surgery to remove her spleen. Alone, almost three thousand miles from home, she found herself being wheeled down a hospital corridor, the words of the Jesus Prayer ("Lord Jesus Christ, Son of God, have mercy on me") echoing in her soul:

I knew that once I went under the anesthetic I might not come out of it, not in this life. I was not afraid. The Jesus Prayer was still with me, a strong rope to which I held like a sailor fallen from a ship. If God was ready for the curtain to come down on this final act of my life's drama, I was as ready as I was ever going to be. I am grateful for that feeling of readiness, for the lack of fear, for the assurance that whatever happened all would be well.[1]

"But all shall be well," wrote the fourteenth-century Christian mystic, Lady Julian of Norwich; "and all shall be well, and all manner of thing shall be well."[2] It's a refrain that Madeleine reiterated, time and time again, in her writing and in her life.[3] Many years earlier, when her nine-year-old granddaughter Léna had been hit, as a pedestrian, by a truck in July of 1977, Madeleine was awed by the miracle of people praying, all over the country, for that little girl—not just people like her good friend Luci but total strangers. Yet Madeleine knew that prayers did not guarantee the hoped-for outcome. She wrote in *Walking on Water*, "The largest part of that act of thanksgiving was gratitude for my children and grandchildren, for the first nine years of Léna's life, and then to say with Lady Julian of Norwich, 'But all shall be well' . . . and then to add, 'No matter what.' That was the important part, the 'no matter what.'"[4] Whatever the outcome, Madeleine would cling to the goodness and mercy of God.

Léna survived her accident. Years later, Madeleine survived her own. But Madeleine knew such happy endings were not a foregone conclusion. She was no stranger to loss, to things being not well, as story after story from her early life demonstrates:

As a young teen, for instance, while staying with her parents and maternal grandmother ("Dearma") at the grandmother's beloved beach cottage near Jacksonville, Florida, Madeleine somehow intuited, late at night, that Dearma was dying. Madeleine woke her parents, and together they went into Dearma's room, where indeed, the old woman was barely breathing. They sat with Dearma, keeping vigil, till she breathed her last.

At age seventeen, Madeleine somehow knew that when she said goodbye to her father on a train platform on the way to boarding school, it would be the last time she would see him. His failing lungs succumbed to pneumonia within months. Urgently summoned to Jacksonville, Florida, where he was hospitalized, she prayed on the train, "Please, God, do whatever is best for Father. Please, do whatever is best."[5] She arrived too late. His death left a hole in her heart and in her life that would never be filled.

Then a close friend committed suicide when Madeleine was a young woman—a devastating act that left Madeleine bewildered and frightened, never able to fully recover from feeling blindsided that anyone would choose to not *be*.

After Madeleine met Hugh in 1944 during the theater production of Anton Chekhov's *The Cherry Orchard* and the two began dating, Hugh suddenly, unaccountably withdrew. For *six months*. "I can remember that Hugh's turning away hurt agonizingly," she would write in *Two-Part Invention*, "and that even in my pain I knew that I would wait for Hugh to come back to me."[6] Then he returned, just as suddenly, as if nothing had happened. She would never name that experience as a kind of betrayal, but when her fictional character Mac similarly abandons Camilla in Madeleine's 1996 novel *A Live Coal in the Sea*, it's not hard to imagine the author working through old, unresolved wounds.

After their marriage, Madeleine and Hugh's adopted daughter, Maria, came to the family in 1956 at age seven after a series of tragedies involving the early deaths of several of the Franklins' friends. Maria would write in *Mothers and Daughters* (coauthored with Madeleine), "My new mother, also shocked by the untimely death of her dear friend, suddenly found herself a mother of three children instead of two. Thus, ours has been a stormy relationship."[7] Even without Madeleine's unwelcome fictionalization of that experience in *Meet the Austins*, one can only imagine how such a deep trauma affected them both.

During the summer of 1971, Madeleine's own mother declined at home with the Franklins, sinking further and further into dementia. In a moment of bewilderment, her mother confessed to feeling afraid; and Madeleine found herself holding and comforting her with the words, "It's all right, Mother. It's all right." Madeleine recounted in *The Summer of the Great-Grandmother*:

> I mean these words. I do not understand them, but I mean them. Perhaps one day I will find out what I mean. They are implicit in everything I write . . . They are behind everything, the cooking of meals, walking the dogs, talking with the girls. I may never find out with my intellectual self what I mean, but if I am given enough glimpses perhaps these will add up to enough so that my heart will understand. It does not; not yet.[8]

Still later, after Hugh died of cancer in 1986, Madeleine claimed, "When my husband died, we didn't have any leftover garbage. We'd gone through the stuff. We were in a good place. And that made grief a lot easier. Still great grief, but very few regrets. And I feel very blessed because of that."[9] Even in the midst of that loss, Madeleine insisted on a kind of happy ending.

Her insistence that "all shall be well" might be yet another example of Madeleine attempting to manipulate the narrative of her life into the kind of story she preferred. Or rather, maybe it's of a piece with her claim that God will not fail with any part of his creation: "For the happy ending," she wrote in *The Rock That Is Higher*, "is intrinsic to the life of faith, central to all we do during all of our lives. If we cannot believe in it, we are desolate indeed. If we know, in the depths of our hearts, that God is going to succeed, with each one of us, with the entire universe, then our lives will be bright with laughter, love, and light."[10]

A light so lovely, yet again. But, as she well knew, we must also reckon with the darkness.

● ● ● ●

Madeleine was no denier of the existence of evil. In fact, one could argue that more than any other writer of children's fiction, she named evil for what it is—a demonic presence at war with God—and empowered her characters to fight it. As L'Engle scholar Don Hettinga writes, "She recognizes that evil sometimes appears under the guise of good, that, as she repeatedly reminds readers, the devil often masquerades as an angel of light. In fact," he adds, "the plots of the books in the Time Trilogy are built to some degree on that assumption."[11]

Which of us, when reading *A Wind in the Door* (1973), for instance, doesn't shiver at Meg Murry's chance encounter with her sworn enemy, principal Mr. Jenkins, in a field behind the house at dusk—a Mr. Jenkins who, when startled, "rose up into the night like a great, flapping bird, [and] flew, screaming across the sky, became a rent, an emptiness, a slash of nothingness—"?[12] He wasn't Mr. Jenkins, of course; he was an "Echthroi," a demonic projection, an image so creepy and startling that we forget we're reading a children's book.

"How many of us call the devil by name today?" Madeleine wrote in *Walking on Water*. "If we see God's love manifested for us in the Incarnation, the life and death and resurrection of Jesus, then we need to also recognize the malignant force that would try to destroy God's love in a particular way, too." Ever the student of literature, she argued, "The antagonist in a story or play is never vague or general; there is always a person behind the forces of evil; otherwise we will not take them seriously . . ."[13]

For Madeleine, the devil is real; evil has a personality; it's gathering power across the universe; it's actively at work to smother and obliterate the light. The battle between light and darkness is not some kind of abstract imbalance that needs to be recalibrated: it's war.

Don Hettinga told me, "I can't think of many other children's novels published prior to *Wrinkle*—other than, of course, the Narnia series or, perhaps, something by George MacDonald—that so clearly delineated good and evil. Shortly after *Wrinkle*, though, we see more—Lloyd Alexander's Chronicles of Prydain and Susan Cooper's Dark is Rising Sequence, both appeared in the mid-sixties." And by the mid-'90s, of course, Harry Potter had arrived at Hogwarts for one of the biggest showdowns between good and evil in all of recent literature. The enemy in J. K. Rowling's series is referred to in whispers, by most characters, as "He-Who-Must-Not-Be-Named"; but Harry dares to say the enemy's name aloud, *Voldemort*, and in that naming we hear echoes of Madeleine L'Engle again. Call evil what it is, Madeleine insisted. Even, and perhaps especially, for children.

Let's not forget the Anglican-Episcopal tradition into which she was baptized. The baptismal rite from the 1892 edition of the Book of Common Prayer instructs the presiding minister to tell the parents of the child candidate (sternly, we can imagine, in a voice not unlike Mrs Which's), "I demand therefore: Dost thou, in the name of this Child, renounce the devil and all his works, the vain pomp and glory of the world, with all covetous desires of the same, and the sinful desires of the flesh, so that thou wilt not follow, nor be led by them?" To which the (somewhat startled) parents are to answer, "I renounce them all; and, by God's help, will endeavor not to follow, nor be led by them." In keeping with those bold, vibrant words of the liturgy, Madeleine could dare to call evil what it was. She could look at something like nuclear war, for instance, and say, in effect, "But *that* is not of Christ. That's evil. That's Satan at work. And I renounce it."

Ultimately, for Madeleine, the love of God in Christ is more powerful than evil and will outlast all things. *"And the light shineth in the darkness,"* says Mrs Who in that pivotal moment in *A Wrinkle in Time*; *"and the darkness comprehended it not."*[14] As we noted earlier, the quote is from the first chapter of John's gospel (1:5)—"John who speaks most closely to my understanding," Madeleine described him, "who helps put the mind in the heart to bring wholeness."[15] And Madeleine loved that word, *comprehend*, which extends also to the older meaning: to encompass, overtake, overcome. The darkness does not overcome the light but rather the reverse.

And how? "Jesus!" Charles Wallace replies, in that Sunday school answer to which those of us steeped in irony roll our eyes. But Madeleine was dead earnest.

Picture the bold minister again, glancing up at the congregation with glasses that look suspiciously like Mrs Who's. He prays stridently from the 1892 baptismal rite: "Grant that *this Child* may have power and strength to have victory"—and everyone, even the people who slipped in the back late, strain to glimpse the baby's round face—"and to triumph, against the devil, the world, and the flesh." Wide-eyed, the parents and the people respond, *"Amen."*

Dare we pray such prayers for today's children? Dare we name aloud the enemy they're up against? Dare we claim that God will not fail with any part of his creation? that in Christ, light and goodness eclipse darkness and evil, now and forever?

Dare we say with the congregation—with Madeleine herself—*Amen?*

● ● ● ●

Madeleine's detractors didn't see her message this way. They charged her with dangerously misleading children by presenting a kind of yin-yang balance between light and dark.[16] And certainly at times she spoke of darkness as a natural part of creation (God creates it in Genesis 1:4–5, after all), a good gift for our own rest and healing, even part of our own subconscious—her 1977 Wheaton College commencement address was about this very topic.[17] But the natural darkness that God created is not the same as the spiritual darkness of evil that seeks to annihilate. Such nuance was lost on her critics, who relied heavily on special knowledge of New Age philosophy to base their arguments. Without insight into the occult, they claimed, it was possible that "in the minds of good but naïve Christian families the ground is being prepared to accept a spiritually disastrous philosophy."[18] They insisted that unless you knew this information, you didn't have a true understanding of Scripture and would be easily deceived.

Let me say this frankly: such reliance on special wisdom sounds like a modern-day form of Gnosticism, an ancient Greek philosophy that seeped into the early church. *Gnosis* is Greek for "wisdom," and Gnostics believed you couldn't truly follow Jesus unless you had their secret knowledge of "higher things"—one of many heresies against which the apostle Paul may have been arguing in his letter to the Colossians and which was denounced by church leaders such as Saint Irenaeus in the second century.[19]

Gnosticism hasn't gone away, obviously; it's just taken different forms. I once found myself on a twelve-hour drive with an old friend who fervently insisted that a certain conspiracy-theorist podcaster had *the* only correct interpretation of end times Scriptures—and that I was potentially in danger if I didn't know about the podcaster, his books, and his teachings. I gently pushed back, asking my friend if he thought the podcaster's knowledge was more powerful than the Holy Spirit, in whose name I was baptized and confirmed and whose presence Jesus promised his followers. After all, the resurrected Jesus told his disciples in Acts 1:7–8, "It is not for you to know the times or dates the Father has set by his own authority. But you will receive power when the Holy Spirit comes on you." The good news is not special insider information only available by joining some kind of exclusive club; by God's grace it's accessible to all.

"And it's free," I said. "How much does that guy charge you?"

It was a long twelve hours.

Not to dismiss the active presence of evil trying to twist our understanding (Madeleine certainly didn't). But her detractors' obsession with knowledge of the occult and the demonic raises the question of whether we really trust the power of Jesus to be stronger than the powers of darkness. Is the Holy Spirit really bound in a straightjacket? Does the Devil really deserve all this air time—more air time than Jesus? What happens to our souls when we spend so much energy focused in that direction? Madeleine said of one censor, "I truly feared for this woman. We find what we are looking for. If we are looking for life and love and openness and growth, we are likely to find them. If we are looking for witchcraft and evil, we'll likely find them, and we may get taken over by them."[20]

In the early 1990s the book *Trojan Horse: How the New Age Movement Infiltrates the Church*, by Brenda Scott and Samantha Smith, accused L'Engle of an insidious conspiracy under the guise of Christianity. The book was, in Madeleine's estimation, a personal attack, a "character assassination" that left her devastated and defensive. And not being judgmental was a tremendous quandary for Madeleine. During the Q&A for her plenary "The Cosmic Questions" at the 1996 Festival of Faith and Writing, she reiterated:

We do tend to find what we look for. And not enough people are looking for Christ. I don't understand Christians who are looking for hate. That is not Christlike. But, see, I have a real big problem here: How do I keep from being judgmental about people I think are judgmental? [audience laughter] But it does make me very sad. Because when I write something which I believe is an offering to God and it's seen as wicked, I say, "What have I done wrong? Is it . . . is it really . . . is that what the book says?" But then I get enough affirmation from other people saying, "No, that's not what the book says." There's something abroad today that frightens me that I've never seen before, in a group of people calling themselves Christians who want to put other Christians down, rather than uphold, teach, be witnesses.

Don Hettinga's scholarly work *Presenting Madeleine L'Engle* came out shortly after *Trojan Horse*, and in it he affirmed the Christian themes in Madeleine's writing. Madeleine, for her part, claimed that Don's book "[gave] me back my life again."[21] He then came under attack himself in Claris Van Kuiken's 1996 book *Battle to Destroy Truth: Unveiling a Trail of Deception*—an exhaustive account of Van Kuiken's four-year battle with the pastor and elders of her local Christian Reformed Church of America over the church's refusal to denounce what she felt was L'Engle's anti-biblical theology.

An online description of Van Kuiken says, "For over 25 years, Mrs. Van Kuiken has been researching and exposing the many ways in which New Age/occult beliefs and practices are penetrating America, its churches and Christian schools—under the guise of being 'Christian.'" It's worth noting that by contrast, the apostle Paul—arguably the best educated of all the apostles—wrote to the Christians at Corinth, "And so it was with me, brothers and sisters. When I came to you, I did not come with eloquence or human wisdom as I proclaimed to you the testimony about God. For I resolved to know nothing while I was with you except Jesus Christ and him crucified . . . so that your faith might not rest on human wisdom, but on God's power" (1 Corinthians 2:1–5). Whenever someone insists on anything extra, proceed with caution.

In such experiences, compassion becomes yet another key Christian practice. I wrote to Don of Madeleine's opponents, "I can't imagine what it's like to live inside an unjoyful reality where the power of Satan is so much stronger than the Holy Spirit, where the ramifications of Adam's choice are more lasting than the ramifications of Jesus's victory, and where the truth sets no one free." Don wrote back, "I wished that these attackers could see Madeleine as a person; if they did, if they read her books with care or if they encountered her in real life, they would have discovered her to be a person of integrity and strong faith." His graciousness reminded me that our first, most loving response to anyone with whom we disagree should be to pray for these brothers and sisters.

Don's careful attention to Madeleine's work, and her reciprocal gratitude, "pointed to the necessarily collective nature of our responses to unreason," he told me. This is how we cling to the mercy and goodness of God: not alone, to be picked off by our own fears (if not by actual opponents), but *together*, as fellow believers who help to bear one another's burdens when all feels dark. "Like it or not, we either add to the darkness of indifference and out-and-out evil which surround us or we light a candle to see by," Madeleine wrote.[22] We must not be so foolish as to dismiss the darkness: it's real. And together we must cling to the truth that the light of Christ will have the last word. This is our communal hope.

● ● ● ●

Evil isn't just "out there," in the forces that seek to deceive and bind. It's in our own souls too. It's here in our own fears and challenges, our sinful tendencies, our painful histories and relationships. "As we think about this vast, cosmic battle, it is far too easy to fall into dualism," Madeleine wrote in *And It Was Good*, "to think of darkness and light battling each other from the beginning, as some of the eastern religions proclaim. But if God created everything and saw that it was good, then something must have happened to this good, to change and distort it." She continued, "The problem is not from without; it rose from within. And we have within each of us some of this wrongness, and too often we refuse to see it, and don't understand why we are not happy, nor why our faith seems a dim thing, nor why our prayers are like dead ashes."[23]

I can't help thinking of Meg's paralyzing, powerful anger at her father, in *Wrinkle*, for rescuing her and Calvin but failing to save Charles Wallace, whom he left behind in the evil of the planet Camazotz. Meg may be temporarily safe on another planet, lovingly attended by the healing character called Aunt Beast, but the darkness of Camazotz is still there, in Meg's own heart, in her fury at her father, in her terror at having left Charles Wallace alone, imprisoned, on a distant planet.

We may wish to locate evil outside of ourselves, as something else to blame, when in fact it's right here, corroding us from the inside out.

Throughout Madeleine's own life, she knew this darkness, particularly in relationships, only too well. When her son Bion died in 1999, here was a story Madeleine couldn't script the way she wanted it to be. Here was a painful chapter for which there was no resolution. No matter how she spun it, this would never be well.

Luci described it to me this way: "Her son Bion had this love/hate relationship with his mother. He was a very difficult person. One of the reasons I was able to be close to Madeleine was that Bion liked me and thought that I was a good influence on his mother." Luci recalled, "Madeleine and I were together with Bion at the point of his death, right at the moment of his death. We were in the hospice room with him, and I think I was the last person to actually lift a glass of water with a straw in it for him to take a sip. And we listened to his breathing just diminish and diminish. And she said, 'You know, a mother shouldn't see her son die.'"

In the aftermath, Luci says, "there was a huge amount of mourning, I think particularly because a lot of issues between them hadn't been resolved. And it seemed like she realized it was never going to be resolved because there's no longer an opportunity for interaction."

Madeleine's granddaughter Charlotte concurs: "The grief over Bion's death was her undoing. Absolutely. She was so sad and didn't take joy in the same things in the same way. The grief contributed to cognitive decline which also makes things harder. He died of end-stage alcoholism. His liver failed. And it's a really ugly death. We were all in denial about it. Not just her." Charlotte described how, once the family had a diagnosis, they could make a way forward with some relief. Everyone except Madeleine.

"I don't think it was anything she was able to accept," Charlotte told me. "He was always Rob Austin for her, this golden, precocious boy with adorable language play. I don't think there was a way for her to talk and write about that. And I think she really bumped up against privacy: how do you respect his privacy? How do you do this without exploiting your child?"

In one of the rare, high-profile public interviews Madeleine did after her son died (for PBS in 2000), she read aloud from her journal, "Bion's death has ripped the fabric of the universe." She then told her interviewer, Bob Abernethy, "In times when we are not particularly suffering we do not have enough time for God. We are too busy with other things. And then the intense suffering comes and we can't be busy with other things. And then God comes into the equation. 'Help.' And we should never be afraid of crying out 'Help' . . . When there is no suffering, nothing happens."[24]

I'm reminded of Mother Teresa's painful letters in her posthumous collection *Come Be My Light: The Private Writings of the "Saint of Calcutta."* The collection was almost never published—not merely because she had requested that her writings remain private, but because they chart her fifty-year journey with a devastating sense of God's absence, of continual darkness. It began almost as soon as Mother Teresa established the Missionaries of Charity in Calcutta in the mid-1940s, after which she would write to her archbishop, "Pray for me—for within me everything is icy cold.—It is only that blind faith that carries me through for in reality to me all is darkness."[25] A decade into this burden she experienced a strange turning point: "For the first time in this 11 years—I have come to love the darkness.—For I believe now that it is a part, a very, very small part of Jesus' darkness and pain on earth."[26] For Mother Teresa, the pain never lifted. The journey would last, without reprieve, until her death half a century later.

Madeleine wrote, "As Gregory of Nyssa points out, when Moses first talked with God, he talked in the light, but as he grew in spiritual stature he talked with God in the darkness. But what darkness!"[27] Luci Shaw told me, "We have times of stagnation and we have a further leap of faith. It's not just a steady growth in God." Charlotte agreed: "I've been thinking about the way we talk about our lives as a journey, and that death is maybe the end. Except where you are at the end maybe says more than you want it to about what your journey has been about unless you end on an *up* note. It's depressing, the oppressive expectations of things getting better: you will get wiser, you will get kinder, you will get calmer as you go down the one road that you are on—as if it's one road in one direction all the time."

For Charlotte, "I think it's liberating, too, not to try to shake that narrative off. Like, 'Oh, I've learned so much toward my journey toward adulthood; and now I am a wise old woman, and people come to me for advice, and I dispense advice, and nothing new happens to me.' To realize that getting older doesn't mean things stop happening to you, yet continuing to remain open to those as intense experiences—it's not easy for us to allow for that in our idols."

On stage with Luci at the 1996 Festival of Faith and Writing,

Madeleine described her accident in California: "I was half dead in the hospital and Luci was—you were in Europe, weren't you?" Luci murmured assent, and Madeleine continued, "And when she came home she simply got on a plane and flew to San Diego and came to the hospital and stayed with me. That's friendship. I was a total mess. Why I was alive, I don't even know. And Luci was . . . I couldn't hold the Bible, she read the psalms for me, and just helped pull me back into life." Madeleine concluded, "Without these real testaments of friendship I wouldn't be here . . . All of the old primordial fears surfaced in me . . . I didn't want to be enclosed . . . I was afraid of the dark . . . And it was a long time before I could sleep without a nightlight on and rejoice in the dark again."

We never stop growing and changing, facing down our fears, confronting new ones. Even when our own hearts grow dark, we need the loving presence of friends and companions to draw us back to the light.

● ● ● ●

In the face of irrational evil, of the darkness that penetrates even our own souls, "believing," Meg says in *A Wind in the Door*, "takes practice." Charlotte told me that her grandmother "described *A Wrinkle in Time* as a sort of aspirational story, writing about a universe in which she hoped to believe. 'All shall be well and all manner of things shall be well' is an aspiration," Charlotte said. "I think of that quote, 'Some days I hold onto my faith with my fingernails'—and that's just sometimes how it is."

Yet even in Madeleine's seasons of doubt, she still prayed

and read her Bible nearly every night. "No matter where I am, at home, abroad, I begin the day with morning prayer [from the Book of Common Prayer], including the psalms for the day, so that at the end of each month I have gone through the book of Psalms. I also read from both the Old and New Testaments . . . I end the day in the same way, with evening prayer, and this gives the day a structure."[28]

When asked about the spiritual practices Barbara Braver and Madeleine did together as apartment mates for those twelve years after Hugh died, Barbara explained, "We lived as persons of sacrament, of 'outward and visible sign': the candles on the table, the effort to make a meal, the comfort food, the sacraments and rituals." One of those rituals was nightly Compline, which Madeleine referred to as the "Go-to-Bed-Quietly-and-Fearlessly Office." Barbara told me that, "Madeleine said more than once, 'Well. Monks, you know, they often lie down to do this.' So she would quite often insist that she was going to lie down to pray, but was vigorous nonetheless." Barbara chuckled at the thought. "And we loved to sing. Every now and then, we'd burst into song. And of course, sometimes we'd come home at different times and both be exhausted and nothing like that would happen at all."

Madeleine herself described Compline as "just this beautiful intimacy with God where they can hear Jesus saying, 'Fear not, little flock. I'm with you. I came because I care. I came because I love you.'" Was it always wonderful and powerful and life-giving? No, Madeleine asserted:

> There are times when I just do it. It doesn't mean any-thing; nothing happens. But I do it. And I think that's

rather like a pianist who goes to practice the scales and does not like doing it. But if you're going to play the Bach fugues you have to practice the scales. And so for me this regular reading of scripture is the practicing of the scales of faith. And I don't have to enjoy it every day— sometimes it's marvelous; I love it! But I have to do it every day whether I like it or not. And it is one of the great building blocks of keeping my faith alive.[29]

Prayer and Bible study weren't a magic formula that would fix everything. But she chose to practice it anyway, because "I knew only that I was lost and that I needed to be found."[30]

Thus, when she encountered people who likewise felt lost, her response was prayer. Don said of her 1996 Calvin College visit, "She was in a wheelchair because of a leg injury, and as her companion wheeled her into a very small elevator, a woman approached her to thank her for her writing about the death of her husband in *Two-Part Invention*. It meant a lot, the woman said, because she had recently been diagnosed with cancer. L'Engle's response was to roll out of the elevator, grasp the woman's hand, and to pray with her for healing."

Madeleine also attended worship whenever she was able, where taking the sacrament of Communion was a particularly poignant way to let in the light of Christ. When her own mother was dying, Madeleine's son-in-law Alan, an Episcopal priest, or Canon West would celebrate the sacrament with the family, "and from this I receive the same kind of strength which, in a different way, comes to me in the C minor Fugue, and I am able to return to the routine of these difficult days with a lighter touch."[31] A decade later, when Hugh was dying, she regularly took Communion then too: "It is by these holy mysteries that I live, that I am sustained."[32]

But it's not only in spiritual practices that we find ourselves able to put one foot in front of the other; it's also in the simple, daily practices of ordinary living. Incarnational practices, we might call them—by which we claim that God shows up in our everyday activities like eating and washing and conversing and winding down at the end of the day.

One of Madeleine's editors, Sandra Jordan, once asked her at a writer's conference how she could withstand "all that intensity, the overwhelming tide of people wanting something from her, needing something beyond a book signed or a comment about their manuscript, needing a spiritual connection." Madeleine's response was, "I have a rule. At 9:00 p.m., I go to my room no matter what, and I'm done for the day."[33] Similarly, Charlotte told me about Madeleine's practice of opening the many shutters that lined the windows of her Manhattan apartment bedroom every morning and then ceremonially closing them all at night. The simple routines of letting the light in at dawn and then saying goodbye to the day—these were yet another way to practice faith in the God who made it all—day, night, sun, moon, and stars—and called them *good*.

I've already discussed how writing was, for Madeleine, a spiritual discipline, one of the ways that she experienced the presence of God. One wonders how her inability to write in those later years, during her decline, affected her sense of drawing near to God, of God drawing near to her. She had written in *Walking on Water*, "It is not easy for me to be a Christian, to believe twenty-four hours a day all that I want to believe. I stray, and then my stories pull me back if I listen to them carefully. I have often been asked if my Christianity affects my stories, and surely it is the other way around; my stories affect my Christianity, restore me, shake me by the scruff of the neck, and pull this straying sinner into an awed faith."[34] But what happens when you can no longer write your way to clarity or peace or even belief? Where is God in the midst of that terrifying vocational silence?

As I was tracking the timeline of her publications, I noticed that she wrote nothing of real significance after Bion's death. Yet in her interview with Bob Abernethy of PBS in 2000 she said she planned to write someday about the loss of her son.

"Did she?" I asked Charlotte.

"As far as I know she never wrote about his death," Charlotte reflected. "She did keep writing, and she was sort of writing two books towards the end: a book about Meg in her forties and a book about aging. But she never got very far with them." Madeleine's physical and mental decline also coincided with that time, Charlotte said, and "I think as different kinds of capacities began to stale, that was really hard. But even towards the last, the scraps of a journal entry on a yellow pad, or the beginning of a poem, were things that surfaced and spoke to her. But I think it must have been terrible not to have that outlet."

At the same time, Charlotte reflected, "I didn't observe her being in distress about not writing. When people would ask her, she had the answer: she would say, 'I am writing a book about aging and Meg in her forties.' That didn't change even if she wasn't actively writing about it. That's so much of who she was, that's what she said. She kept her prayer book and her Bible at her bedside."

Madeleine taught us that we don't abandon spiritual habits just because we're in a season of struggle and doubt. We keep attending to those practices, day in and day out. This is not the same as legalism, in which we obey certain commands in some misguided attempt to be on God's good side. Instead, it requires deep humility and trust to acknowledge, "I don't understand this right now. Everything feels dark and meaningless. But there's more going on than I understand; and somehow God has promised to show up in the midst of these daily habits. So here goes." Prayer, worship, reading Scripture, breaking bread in community, spiritual counsel, and conversation with spiritual friends: all those are ways we put one foot in front of the other, even in the dark. These are the ways we practice believing.

● ● ● ●

In the early part of the eight years between Bion's death and her own, Madeleine split her time between New York and the cottage she'd had built at Crosswicks, near the big farmhouse. Eventually, however, the stretches of time in each place grew longer. "And in between," Charlotte said, "she'd fall and her hip would dislocate and at one point she had a pretty significant brain hemorrhage." After one particularly bad fall the family moved her into a nursing home in Litchfield, Connecticut, and there she spent the last few years of her life.

Luci and Barbara together went to visit her. Luci recalls, "The thing that was important for me and Barbara was right at the end, when Madeleine was in an elder-care place. She had really lost her memory and she was unable to communicate. She couldn't respond to anything we said." But then, Luci says, "We started to sing a hymn—you know, we'd always do Compline together when it was the three of us; we would sing a hymn at the end of Compline together—and as soon as we started singing this hymn, she joined in. It was an underlying current in her memory that the music and the words broke open again." Luci then asked the home staff to contact her if Madeleine was ever alert enough for a phone call, and not long thereafter, they were able to have a lucid conversation across the miles between Connecticut and the West Coast.

Two weeks later, Madeleine was gone.

Luci, ever the poet, painted that last scene for us all:

TO THE EDGE
for Madeleine L'Engle

Be with her now. She faces the ocean
of unknowing, losing the sense
of what her life has been, and soon

will be no longer as she knew it, as
we knew it with her. Lagging behind,
we cannot join her on this nameless shore.

Knots in her bones, flesh flaccid, the skin
like paper, pigment gathering like ashes driven
by a random wind, a heart

that may still sing, interiorly—we cannot
know—have pulled her far ahead of us,
our pioneer.

As we embrace her, her inner eyes embrace
the universe. She recognizes heaven with its
innumerable stars—but not our faces.

Be with her now, *as you have*
sometimes been—a flare that blazes,
then dulls, leaving only a bright

blur in the memory. Hold her
in the mystery that no one can describe
but Lazarus, though he was dumb

and didn't speak of it. Fog has rolled in,
erasing definition at the edge. Walking
to meet it, she hopes soon to see

where the shore ends. She listens as
the ocean breathes in and out in waves.
She hears no other sound.[35]

●　　●　　●　　●

Despite the darkness, Barbara Braver concluded, "Madeleine showed up. Maybe we can write a little chapter called 'Madeleine Showed Up.' She did. She showed up to people who needed her when they needed her, she showed up for prayer, she showed up to let the voice of inspiration speak." Madeleine showed up to serve the work of writing; she disciplined herself to sit down and be present. And she showed up as a struggling believer; she disciplined herself to continue praying, continue reading the Bible, continue practicing hospitality, continue worshiping in community. She perhaps never wrested every chapter of her life into a tidy resolution in which "all shall be well," but she put her trust in the One whose love does not fail.

We can picture it in our mind's eye, Madeleine's bedside table with her prayer book and her Bible. Many of us have a similar table, piled with books, maybe, or photos of loved ones. Is our prayer book there too, tabbed to Compline? Is the Bible there, that complex, bewildering, life-giving book Madeleine taught us to read as we read our favorite childhood stories? Because the kinds of things on our bedside table today most likely will not change in forty years. "How we spend our days," wrote author Annie Dillard, "is, of course, how we spend our lives."[36] We won't magically become more spiritually disciplined in old age if we're not practicing now.

So it starts tonight. It starts with the closing of the shutters against the darkness. It starts with our determination to go to bed quietly and fearlessly, talking to God about our day. Then, when dawn comes, we can arise like Madeleine, open the shutters, and let in the light so lovely, whether we feel like it or not.

EPILOGUE: TESSER WELL

If the Word of God is the light of the world, and this light cannot be put out, ultimately it will brighten all the dark corners of our hearts and we will be able to see, and seeing, will be given the grace to respond with love—and of our own free will.

The Irrational Season

When Catholic writer Jessica Mesman Griffith (*Love and Salt*) was fourteen, her mother died of cancer. "And that," Jessica said to me when I interviewed her for this book, "ended life as I knew it."

Jessica had grown up Catholic in New Orleans, but when her mom got sick her parents grew "desperate for a faith healing," so they became involved in a nondenominational Pentecostal church. The family left Catholicism; and when Jessica's mother died her father quickly remarried someone from that church. "Which meant that everything that was familiar to me was gone: my Catholic faith, my mother."

And she was not allowed to grieve. "My life took on the feeling of an alternate reality."

Madeleine L'Engle's *A Wrinkle in Time* became a key story for her. "I became really, really troubled, a rebellious teenager, very stubborn, very angry. Which are listed as all of Meg's faults. Mrs Whatsit gives Meg her faults as a way to fight the darkness. Looking back, I think I could've become something worse—suicidal, addicted. But I was determined to survive, almost as an affront to my dad."

Years later, after her own marriage had begun falling apart, Jessica was persuaded to return to Louisiana and attempt reconciliation with her father. She said, "I packed up my two young children and put them in a car and drove nineteen hours home. And the whole way we were listening to *A Wrinkle in Time* audiobook, narrated by Hope Davis—in its entirety several times." But things in Louisiana quickly deteriorated. "I saw that, no, this was exactly the reason why I left; I was right to leave. This is a toxic place to me. There is no home where suddenly everything is better."

She packed up the children again, uncertain of where to go. "I was driving around the dark streets at night. It was raining, cold, and dreary. And we were just driving around because listening to the book was the only thing my kids wanted to do." Then suddenly, she became aware of what the book was saying. It was chapter ten, "Absolute Zero," when Meg has barely survived her father's attempt to tesser them away from Camazotz.

"She had found her father," came Hope Davis's voice, "and he had not made everything all right."

"In that moment," Jessica explained, "I pulled over and thought, 'This could be it for me. This could be the thing that I don't survive.' And I realized I could let it consume me; I could let it push me down into hate. Or I can fight through it for these kids. Find a way. And then I remembered my faults, my stubbornness."

She recalled, "It was a horrible, horrible night. It was the darkest night of my life. And yet feeling that pain, allowing myself to feel that pain, that anger, that betrayal I felt by so many of the people who were supposed to take care of me . . . that was the beginning of healing."

For Jessica, *Wrinkle* has been "the touchstone, again and again, in different phases. But to have it speak to me on that level at that moment . . . there was just something cosmic about it. So I feel like I, in some way, owe L'Engle my life."

●   ●   ●   ●

"My daughter," Dr. Murry tells Meg after they escape from Camazotz to the planet Ixchel without Charles Wallace, "I am not a Mrs Whatsit, a Mrs Who, or a Mrs Which . . . I am a human being, and a very fallible one. But I agree with Calvin. We were sent here for something. And we know that all things work together for good to them that love God, to them who are the called according to his purpose."[1]

It's one of many places in *Wrinkle* where characters directly quote the Bible—in this case, Romans 8:28. Madeleine used the King James Version (KJV), her favorite—although it's worth noting that other versions simply weren't common back in the early '60s. But since then, other versions translate Romans 8:28 as "all things God works for the good of those who love him." This could be easily misread as saying that God manipulates circumstances on our behalf, which makes God out to be our personal magic genie. The KJV, however, suggests that no matter our circumstances, our love for God and trust in God's calling become the twin lenses by which we are able to see God's hand at work.

Our actual events, on the ground, haven't changed. What *has* changed is us.

At that moment in *Wrinkle*, Meg is so angry at her father that she is "as much in the power of the Black Thing as Charles Wallace."[2] All she can see is terror and panic and loss. The only thing that will lift her out of that terror is her love for her little brother and for the father she feels has failed her. Her circumstances may not change, but she is part of a larger dance, the good cosmic design that God has created. This turnaround will not happen by her own power; she will need help from beyond herself—in this case, from a creature on Ixchel that she names "Aunt Beast." It is in relinquishing control to a being who knows her, in many ways, better than she knows herself that Meg begins to heal.

As tempting as it is to think of Madeleine L'Engle as our very own Aunt Beast or even our Mrs Whatsit, Madeleine was, like Dr. Murry, a "human being, and a very fallible one." Her journey was not always one of clarity or even peace. "My spiritual scales fluctuate wildly," she wrote in *The Irrational Season*. "They are always on the heavy side, but there are days when I am able to travel light, and these days show me the way."[3] Those fluctuations were never wilder than when Madeleine was attempting to practice charity and empathy toward others, wrestling with the paradox of loving those we find it difficult to love.

In that same passage of *The Irrational Season,* she tells about worshiping alongside an acquaintance who regularly went to Communion before work every day and yet hated all people of Asian descent. "Surely within me there is an equal blindness," she wrote, "something that I do not recognize in myself, that I justify without even realizing it. All right, brother. Let us be forgiven together, then."[4]

All right, brother, we say to the angry relative at Thanksgiving. *All right, sister,* we say to the person on social media whose politics sound like a foreign language. *All right,* we say to our idols when they disappoint us. *Let us be forgiven together, then.* We will only make a way forward when we recognize that we too are flawed and wounded sojourners, that where we are now on the journey is not the end game.

As Madeleine said at the 1996 Festival of Faith and Writing, "We're supposed to be such witnesses of Christ's love that other people will want to know what makes us glow. And the minute we begin to hate, to put down, that light goes. I know that when I'm angry, I can feel my light flickering and dimming. It's only when I'm willing to let go, and listen . . ."

Decades later, our fraught times demand of us these same daily practices of humility and patience—perhaps more urgently now than ever.

●　　●　　●　　●

Novelist Leif Enger got it right when he called Madeleine L'Engle "an apologist for joy."[5] For Madeleine, the great challenge of the life of faith was letting go of anger and fear and instead embracing joy—indeed, practicing joy as a spiritual discipline. And for many who knew her, this was the single greatest attribute they remember. Said *Wrinkle* film producer Catherine Hand, "Madeleine had this inner joy and faith in all of us, in the universe. That was what was so infectious about her, so inspiring."

I'm reminded of Thomas Bona's comment about Madeleine's "joyful uncertainty." I can't think of a phrase more contrary to the vitriol we hear in cultural discourse today, particularly on social media, where everyone is certain, everyone is earnest, and no one seems particularly happy. Actual lives are at stake, we can't forget. Real people are suffering. But if people of faith are called, as the apostle Paul says, to "mourn with those who mourn," we are also called to "rejoice with those who rejoice" (Romans 12:15). After all, wrote the ancient Israelite leader Nehemiah as his people returned from exile, "The joy of the Lord is your strength" (Nehemiah 8:10).

Madeleine showed us how to rejoice in the smallest atom, the farthest galaxy, all the amazing works of our Creator—and also to rejoice in the creative tasks God has given us to do. We may not be certain about every detail. We may not find satisfying answers to our most haunting questions. We may never see the hoped-for reconciliation between ourselves and the loved ones we've failed—or who've failed us. But for my part, I'll take joyful uncertainty over joyless certainty any day.

The fall of 2018 would've marked Madeleine's one-hundredth birthday. She *loved* birthdays. She would not have wanted us to forget it. Celebration too is a spiritual discipline of joy. But we don't inhabit some kind of eternal Pinterest board, surrounded by inspirational phrases and uncluttered homes and well-behaved children. That sounds just a little too much like Camazotz, actually. Rather, we allow ourselves—and the people we love—to inhabit the complex spaces of difficulty and struggle, because this is what it means to be human, to be individuals. The birthday girl, as much as we love her, is not always going to be the life of the party.

As Madeleine's housemate Barbara told me, "Anyone with as rich and complex an inner life as Madeleine is bound to not just run around giggling all day. Life is complicated. It's not simple. It's a slog sometimes. The more we accept that—that there are great wellsprings of joy and whole rivers of sadness, and they're all there. . . . And in order to make it through, there needs to be some awareness of that reality. You just keep on keeping on."

In thousands of signed copies of *A Wrinkle in Time*, Madeleine wrote the same inscription: "Tesser well." We are like Meg Murry. We're all on a journey requiring transitions that aren't particularly pleasant, traveling from places of familiarity to those of strangeness, from one season of life to another. And the fact is, we will tesser badly. We will get hurt. We will hurt others. Our very last tesser may be the hardest one of all. But Madeleine's inscription is both inspirational—*you can do this*—and aspirational: *someday, by God's grace.*

If we can take this to heart as individuals, we can take this to heart for a new generation. With each hourly headline we find ourselves thrust into what feels like entirely strange planets, sometimes flattened, sometimes lost in undiscernible fog. We don't always keep a solid grip on each other's hands. We fail to love. But in all this, Madeleine's legacy isn't merely something to remember with a sigh of nostalgia: it's a call.

In Madeleine's words, "We need to make people know that

the good news is truly good news. I was chastised because I didn't write for Christians. And I said, 'Well, I don't preach to the choir. I want the good news to spread. I want people to understand that what makes life wonderful and terrible and bearable is God's grace and love and laughter.'"[6]

We are, each of us, called to be icons in the world—not angry, glaring spotlights but, rather, windows through which Christ's light shines. What the world hears as bad news must be made beautiful again, that resounding theme of redemption by a God who loved us enough to become one of us, in all our particularity. Even those who are hardest to love.

We worship a God who does not fail. He did not fail with Madeleine; God will not fail with us.

And that is good news.

ACKNOWLEDGMENTS

Many thanks to Stephanie Smith and the team at Zondervan, not only for brainstorming this book with me but giving me the chance to write it.

To my college roommate, Chloe Couch Richards, for first introducing me to the grown-up works of Madeleine L'Engle and thus understanding me better than I understood myself.

Lisa Ann Cockrel for her enthusiasm, insights, and suggestions.

Charlotte Jones Voiklis for keeping Madeleine's legacy alive for a new generation. Having you as a consultant and cheerleader for this project was pure grace.

All my interview subjects, who allowed me to fumble my way through the art of gleaning pertinent information without overly managing the conversation.

Erin Wasinger, for her research assistance and interview savvy: this couldn't have happened without you. Tabitha Martin, who kept our house from disintegrating into a slovenly, unsanitary pit. My long-suffering family, including my parents and in-laws, who juggled childcare and other issues to make this book possible. What manuscript deadline would be complete without at least one child puking?

And finally, to my husband, Tom, whose love for *Two-Part Invention* is undimmed by my probe into L'Engle's idealization of her otherwise less-than-easy marriage. Thank you for your unfailing love and support, especially in the making of this book.

You are lovely lights, all of you.

NOTES

Introduction

1. Madeleine L'Engle, *A Stone for a Pillow: Journeys with Jacob* (New York: Convergent Books edition, 2017), 72.
2. Madeleine L'Engle, *Walking on Water: Reflections on Faith and Art* (Colorado Springs, CO: A Shaw Book published by WaterBrook Press, 1980, 1998, 2001), 191.
3. Madeleine L'Engle, *The Irrational Season* (New York: Harper One, 1977), 113.
4. It wasn't until I was in the final edits for this project that I found the quote that must've prompted this metaphor. In *A Circle of Friends: Remembering Madeleine L'Engle*, her goddaughter, Cornelia Moore, tells of visiting Madeleine after her stroke and "hearing her say with absolute certainty that during the time she was in a coma, she was a whale swimming with a pod of whales singing whale song hymns" (*Circle of Friends*, 20). Charlotte told me she remembers her grandmother saying something similar.
5. L'Engle, *Walking*, 140–41.
6. From the video recording of a Q&A with Madeleine L'Engle at the Veritas Forum, University of California Santa Barbara, Feb. 9, 1998, accessed May 4, 2018. https://www.youtube.com/watch?v=D0AjelTAcMk.

Chapter 1: Icon *and* Iconoclast

1. Madeleine L'Engle, *A Wind in the Door* (New York: Farrar, Straus & Giroux, 1973. Reprint, New York: Bantam Doubleday Dell Books, 1974), 78.
2. L'Engle, *Walking*, 45.
3. Madeleine L'Engle, *Two-Part Invention: The Story of a Marriage* (HarperSanFrancisco, 1988. Reprinted by arrangement with Farrar, Straus & Giroux), 5.
4. Madeleine L'Engle, *The Summer of the Great-Grandmother* (New York: HarperOne, 1974. Reprinted by arrangement with Farrar, Straus & Giroux), 138.
5. Madeleine L'Engle, "George MacDonald: Nourishment for a Private World" in *More Than Words: Contemporary Writers on the Works That Shape Them*, ed. Philip Yancey and James Calvin Schaap (Grand Rapids, MI: Baker Books, 2002), 152.
6. Charlotte Jones Voiklis and Léna Roy, *Becoming Madeleine: A Biography of the Author of* A Wrinkle in Time *by her Granddaughters* (New York: Farrar, Straus & Giroux, 2018), 46.
7. L'Engle, *Irrational Season*, 100.
8. L'Engle, *Great-Grandmother*, part 2, chapter 4, Kindle edition.
9. Madeleine L'Engle, *A Circle of Quiet* (New York: HarperOne, 1972. Reprinted by arrangement with Farrar, Straus & Giroux), 21.
10. L'Engle, *Quiet*, 22.
11. L'Engle, *More Than Words*, 145.
12. From various tributes in *A Circle of Friends: Remembering Madeleine L'Engle*, ed. Katherine Kirkpatrick (A Circle of Friends publication, 2009), 65 and xvii, respectively.
13. Luci Shaw, "Madeleine L'Engle, Writer and Friend (1918–2007)" in *A Circle of Friends*, 25.
14. Cornelia Duryée Moore, "Madeleine L'Engle, *Anam Chara*" in *A Circle of Friends*, 16, 19.
15. Stephanie Cowell, "Supper with Madeleine" in *A Circle of Friends*, 71–73.
16. Various authors, *A Circle of Friends*, xx, 5, and 80–81.

17. For the history of Westmont College's C. S. Lewis Wardrobe, see http://www.westmont.edu/_academics/departments/english/cs-lewis-wardrobe.html, accessed April 2018.

18. Cowell, *A Circle of Friends*, 74.

19. Madeleine L'Engle and Luci Shaw, *Friends for the Journey* (Vancouver, British Columbia: Regent College Publishing, 2003. First published by Vine Books, 1997), 20.

20. Leonard S. Marcus, *Listening for Madeleine: A Portrait of Madeleine L'Engle in Many Voices* (New York: Farrar, Straus & Giroux, 2012), 198.

21. L'Engle, *Quiet*, 18.

22. L'Engle and Shaw, *Friends for the Journey*, 36.

23. Madeleine L'Engle, commencement address at Wheaton College, IL, May 1977, from the Madeleine L'Engle Papers (SC-3), Wheaton College Special Collections, Wheaton, IL.

24. L'Engle and Shaw, *Friends for the Journey*, 23.

25. Richard Beck, "Notes on the Theology of Icons, Part 4: Reverse Perspective," July 18, 2008, accessed May 5, 2018. http://experimentaltheology.blogspot.com/2008/07/notes-on-theology-of-icons-part-4.html.

26. L'Engle *Quiet*, 18.

27. John 3:30.

Chapter 2: Sacred *and* Secular

1. Madeleine L'Engle deliberately spelled the names of the three "Mrs" without the usual period.

2. Marcus, *Listening*, 14.

3. Marcus, *Listening*, 62.

4. L'Engle, *Walking*, 63.

5. See "The Remarkable Influence of *A Wrinkle in Time*" by Natalie Escobar, *Smithsonian Magazine*, Jan. 2018, accessed May 5, 2018. https://www.smithsonianmag.com/arts-culture/remarkable-influence-wrinkle-in-time-180967509/.

6. From the video recording of a panel discussion held during Macmillan's fiftieth anniversary celebration of *A Wrinkle*

in Time, accessed March 2018. https://www.youtube.com/
watch?v=GU7tC4uHiRU.

7. See L'Engle, *Quiet*, 212.

8. Madeleine L'Engle, as quoted by Terry Mattingly in "Tesser
   Well, Madeleine L'Engle," Sept. 12, 2007, accessed May 5,
   2018. http://www.patheos.com/blogs/tmatt/2007/09/tesser-well
   -madeleine-lengle/.

9. Claris Van Kuiken, "The Gospel of Madeleine L'Engle: More
   Than Just A Wrinkle in Time," May 2017, accessed May 5,
   2018. https://ingridschlueter.files.wordpress.com/2017/06/the
   -gospel-of-madeleine-lengle-4.pdf.

10. Van Kuiken, "The Gospel of Madeleine L'Engle."

11. Madeleine L'Engle, as quoted by Douglas Martin in "Madeleine
    L'Engle, Author of the Classic *A Wrinkle in Time*, Is Dead at 88"
    in *The New York Times*, Sept. 8, 2007, accessed May 5, 2018.
    http://www.nytimes.com/2007/09/08/books/08lengle.html.

12. Duane W. H. Arnold and Robert Hudson, *Beyond Belief: What
    the Martyrs Said to God* (Grand Rapids, MI: Zondervan, 2002),
    135.

13. Carole F. Chase, *Madeleine L'Engle Herself: Reflections on a
    Writing Life* (Colorado Springs, CO: A Shaw Book published
    by WaterBrook Press, 2001), 120.

14. Sara Zarr, from the preface to the 2016 edition of *Walking on
    Water* by Madeleine L'Engle (New York: Convergent Books,
    2016), xii.

15. See sociologist Christian Smith's assessment of the spirituality
    of young adults in his landmark National Study of Youth and
    Religion from *Soul Searching: The Religious and Spiritual Lives
    of American Teenagers* (Oxford University Press, 2005), 165.

16. Amena Brown, interviewed on *Christianity Today's* podcast
    The Calling, "Amena Brown: Art Doesn't Need to be 'Churchy'
    to be Sacred," Episode 58, Nov. 15, 2017, accessed January
    2018. http://www.christianitytoday.com/ct/2017/november
    -web-only/amena-brown-art-doesnt-need-to-be-churchy-to-be
    -sacre.html.

17. L'Engle, *Walking*, 27.
18. Madeleine L'Engle, *And It Was Good: Reflections on Beginnings* (New York: Convergent Books, 1983), 45.
19. Madeleine L'Engle, "Do I Dare Disturb the Universe?" speech presented to the Library of Congress, November 16, 1983, Kindle edition.
20. See, for example, C. S. Lewis's sermon "The Weight of Glory" from *The Weight of Glory and Other Addresses*.
21. This isn't to say that Madeleine never mined back into history: she certainly did in her private reading, including the works of the Byzantine and Cappadocian Fathers such as Gregory of Nyssa and "his brilliant sister, Macrina" (Chase, *Herself*, 150).
22. Donald R. Hettinga, *Presenting Madeleine L'Engle* (New York: Twayne Publishers, 1993), 18.
23. Hettinga, *Presenting*, 16.
24. Marcus, *Listening*, 116.
25. Marcus, *Listening*, 199.
26. Madeleine L'Engle, "Into Your Hands, O Lord, I Commend My Spirit" in *The Best Spiritual Writing 1998*, ed. Philip Zeliski (HarperSanFrancisco, 1998), 156–157.
27. Luci Shaw, *A Circle of Friends*, 30.
28. L'Engle, *Best*, 157.
29. Samantha Smith and Brenda Scott, *Trojan Horse: How the New Age Movement Infiltrates the Church* (Lafayette, LA: Huntington House Publishers, 1993), 60.
30. Madeleine L'Engle, *An Acceptable Time* (New York: Square Fish / Macmillan / Farrar, Straus & Giroux, 1989), 322.
31. L'Engle, *Acceptable Time*, 323.
32. Madeleine L'Engle, "The Cosmic Questions," based on her plenary by that title at the 1996 Calvin College Festival of Faith and Writing, in *Shouts and Whispers: Twenty-One Writers Speak About Their Writing and Their Faith*, ed. Jennifer L. Holberg (Grand Rapids, MI: William B. Eerdmans Publishing Company, 2006), 217.
33. L'Engle, *Shouts*, 218.

34. William Griffin, "Eschaton á la Carte" in *Carnage at Christhaven*, ed. William Griffin (San Francisco: Harper & Row, Publishers, 1989), 8.

35. Griffin, *Christhaven*, 1–2.

36. Robert Siegel, "Without One Plea," in *Christhaven*, 11.

37. Luci Shaw, in the forward to *Suncatcher: A Study of Madeleine L'Engle and Her Writing* by Carole F. Chase (Philadelphia: Innisfree Press, 1995, 1998), 13.

Chapter 3: Truth and Story

1. Madeleine L'Engle, *The Rock That Is Higher: Story as Truth* (Wheaton, IL: Harold Shaw Publishers, 1993), 215.

2. Chase, *Herself*, 170.

3. Madeleine L'Engle, *Mothers and Daughters*, with photography by her adopted daughter Maria Rooney (Kelowna, British Columbia: Northstone Publishing, by arrangement with Harold Shaw Publishers, 1997), 38–39.

4. L'Engle, *More Than Words*, 146.

5. L'Engle *Walking*, 64–65.

6. Madeleine L'Engle, introduction to the Bantam Classic edition of *The Little Princess* by Frances Hodgson Burnett (New York: Bantam Books, 1987), vii.

7. George MacDonald, "The Fantastic Imagination," first published in 1893.

8. C. S. Lewis, from the introduction to *George MacDonald: An Anthology* (1946) by Geoffrey Bles as reprinted in the introduction to *Lilith* (1895) by George MacDonald (Grand Rapids, MI: Wm. B. Eerdmans Publishing Company, 1981), xi.

9. L'Engle, *More Than Words*, 149.

10. And my personal favorite (from one reviewer to my critic): "I'm glad I'm not you."

11. A version of this list first appeared in my article "There and Back Again: Why Hobbits Still Matter for the Hunger Games Generation" in the Nov/Dec 2012 issue of the now-defunct *Immerse Journal: A Journal of Faith, Life, and Youth Ministry*.

It was subsequently reprinted on HarperCollins's C. S. Lewis blog, Dec. 22, 2012, accessed May 5, 2018. http://www.cslewis .com/there-and-back-again-why-hobbits-still-matter-for-the -hunger-games-generation/.

12. J. R. R. Tolkien, "On Fairy-Stories" in *The Tolkien Reader* (New York: Ballantine Books, 1966), 89.

13. C. S. Lewis, "Myth Became Fact" in *God in the Dock: Essays on Theology and Ethics,* ed. Walter Hooper (Grand Rapids, MI: William B. Eerdmans Publishing Company, 1970), 58–59.

14. Chase, *Herself,* 318.

15. L'Engle, *Two-Part Invention,* 193.

16. L'Engle, *Irrational Season,* 114.

17. L'Engle, *More Than Words,* 147.

18. L'Engle, *Rock,* 89.

19. L'Engle, *Rock,* 180.

20. L'Engle, *And It Was Good,* 159.

21. Alasdair MacIntyre, *After Virtue: A Study in Moral Theory* (Notre Dame, IN: University of Notre Dame Press, 1981, 1984, 2007), 216.

22. MacIntyre, *Virtue,* 216.

23. Madeleine seems to have conflated or confused the seventeenth-century poet Sir Thomas Browne with the real author of this poem, T. E. Brown, who first published it in 1893 as "Indwelling" in his book *Old John and Other Poems.*

Chapter 4: Faith *and* Science

1. L'Engle, *Best,* 158.

2. L'Engle, *Best,* 159.

3. L'Engle, *Quiet,* 124.

4. L'Engle, *Quiet,* 125.

5. L'Engle, *Acceptable Time,* 9.

6. L'Engle, *Great-Grandmother,* 123. She's referring to one of the fourth-century Cappadocian fathers, St. Gregory of Nyssa, whose strong hope in the resurrection upon the death of his sister, Macrina, sustained him.

7. L'Engle, *Great-Grandmother*, 130.

8. L'Engle, *Two-Part Invention*, 39.

9. L'Engle, *Two-Part Invention*, 52.

10. Madeleine L'Engle, from the interview "Madeleine L'Engle on Allegory and Prayer" with Cheryl Forbes, *Christianity Today*, June 8, 1979, accessed March 2018. https://www.christianity today.com/ct/2007/septemberweb-only/madeleine-lengle -allegory-prayer-wrinkle-time.html.

11. Madeleine L'Engle, *A Severed Wasp* (New York: Farrar, Straus & Giroux, 1982), Kindle edition.

12. L'Engle, *Walking*, 135.

13. L'Engle, *Wasp*, Kindle.

14. See, for instance, George Harrison's "Albert Einstein: Appraisal of an Intellect" in *The Atlantic*, June 1955 (https://www.the atlantic.com/magazine/archive/1955/06/albert-einstein-appraisal -of-an-intellect/303934/, accessed March 2018) along with related articles in the 1955 archives of *The New Yorker*, *Harper's Magazine*, *Scientific American*, and LIFE—all of which (with the exception of *The Atlantic*) Vicky Austin mentions in *The Moon By Night* as journals her parents read, and which, by extension, I conjecture that the Franklins read in real life.

15. L'Engle, *Best*, 160.

16. L'Engle with Forbes, *Christianity Today*.

17. L'Engle with Forbes, *Christianity Today*.

18. L'Engle, *Irrational Season*, 138.

19. L'Engle, *Irrational Season*, 143.

20. Madeleine L'Engle, introduction to the twenty-fifth anniversary of *A Wrinkle in Time*, bundled with "Do I Dare Disturb the Universe?" Kindle edition.

21. L'Engle, *Walking*, 134.

22. L'Engle, *Walking*, 135–36.

23. L'Engle, *Walking*, 206.

24. "Science Goes to the Movies," CUNY TV, Nov. 30, 2017, accessed Feb. 9, 2018. http://www.cuny.tv/show/sciencegoesto themovies/PR2006302.

25. "What Is 'A Wrinkle In Time'? The Science of the Fifth Dimension," *Inverse,* Jan. 16, 2018, accessed Feb. 9, 2018. https://www.inverse.com/article/34273-wrinkle-in-time-fifth-dimension-tesseract-science.

26. L'Engle, *Irrational Season*, 121.

27. The physician is most likely Patricia (Pat) Collins Cowdery, an old friend from Jacksonville, Florida.

28. L'Engle, "Do I Dare Disturb the Universe?" Kindle edition.

29. "Science Goes to the Movies," CUNY TV.

30. "L'Engle's Fiction Inspired Real Science," National Public Radio's *All Things Considered*, Sept. 8, 2007, accessed Feb. 9, 2018. https://www.npr.org/templates/story/story.php?storyId=14266537.

31. Katherine Paterson, introduction to the fiftieth-anniversary edition of *A Wrinkle in Time* by Madeleine L'Engle (New York: Square Fish / Macmillan / Farrar, Straus & Giroux, 2012) xvi.

32. L'Engle, 1996 Veritas Forum.

33. L'Engle, *Best*, 159.

34. Even the apostle John, at the end of his Gospel, tells us that "Jesus did many other things as well," but "if every one of them were written down, I suppose that even the whole world would not have room for the books that would be written (John 21:25)." The Bible does not claim to give us every single bit of knowledge the universe holds, not even all the miraculous signs of Jesus (again, see John 20:30). But it *does* claim to give us what we need to "believe that Jesus is the Messiah, the Son of God, and that by believing you may have life in his name (John 20:31)." How the writer in me loves this detail! Stick to your thesis. If you set out to paint a faithful, compelling portrait in words, then don't dabble in some other purpose. You're not a court reporter: you're an artist. This is not a science textbook: it's a portrait of someone you love. Keep the main thing the main thing.

35. See Psalm 90:4 and 2 Peter 3:8.

36. Van Kuiken, "The Gospel of Madeleine L'Engle."

37. Natalie Grant, "An Open Letter to Madeleine L'Engle," *McSweeney's* online journal, Jan. 14, 2011, accessed May 5, 2018. https://www.mcsweeneys.net/articles/an-open-letter-to -madeleine-lengle.

38. John Polkinghorne, from a 2005 debate held at Liverpool Cathedral with creation scientist John Mackay, hosted by the BBC's Roger Philips, accessed March 2018. https://www.you tube.com/watch?v=8KlJ7Bt3oxE.

39. Charlotte Jones Voiklis, "The Annual Perseid [sic] Meteor Shower Peaks August 11–12, 2017," Aug. 7, 2017 on Madeleine L'Engle's official website, accessed May 5, 2018. https://www. madeleinelengle.com/the-annual-perseid-meteor-shower-peaks -august-11–12–2017/.

40. This footnote is to remind you, the reader, to pause, pick up your smart phone, and look up the meteor shower. Then put the event on your calendar. It's your Madeleine-inspired assignment for the day.

Chapter 5: Religion *and* Art

1. John Rowe Townsend, *A Sense of Story: Essays on Contemporary Writing for Children* (Philadelphia: Lippincott, 1971), 129; as quoted in Hettinga's *Presenting*, 150.

2. Grant, "Open Letter."

3. Marcus, *Listening*, 95.

4. L'Engle, *Shouts*, 215.

5. Madeleine L'Engle, "A Sky Full of Children," from *Watch for the Light: Readings for Advent and Christmas* (Maryknoll, NY: Orbis Books, paperback edition 2004), 81.

6. L'Engle, *Rock*, 68.

7. Marcus, *Listening*, 74.

8. Marcus, *Listening*, 77.

9. See *Circle of Friends*, 15–16.

10. L'Engle, *Walking*, 235.

11. Leif Enger, foreword to *Penguins and Golden Calves: Icons and Idols in Antarctica and Other Unexpected Places* by

Madeleine L'Engle (Colorado Springs, CO: A Shaw Book published by WaterBrook Press, 1996, 2003), xi.

12. L'Engle, *Walking*, 28.
13. Enger, *Penguins*, xii.
14. L'Engle, *Walking*, 9–10.
15. Chase, *Herself*, 129.
16. Madeleine L'Engle, *A Wrinkle in Time* (New York: Farrar, Straus & Giroux, 1962. Reprint, New York: Bantam Doubleday Dell Books, 1973), 199.
17. G. K. Chesterton, *Orthodoxy,* from *The Collected Works of G.K. Chesterton, Vol. I,* ed. David Dooley (San Francisco: Ignatius Press, 1986), 300.
18. Brown, *The Calling* podcast.
19. L'Engle, *Walking*, 5.
20. L'Engle, *Walking*, 50.
21. Hettinga, *Presenting*, 19–20.

Chapter 6: Fact *and* Fiction

1. L'Engle, *Quiet*, 89.
2. L'Engle, *Quiet*, 90.
3. L'Engle, *Quiet*, 92–93.
4. L'Engle, *Rock*, 94.
5. L'Engle, *Walking*, 197.
6. Marcus, *Listening*, 53.
7. Marcus, *Listening*, 182. C. S. Lewis, incidentally, was likewise accused of ignoring whole swaths of his real history. At least one of his oldest and closest friends, to whom he was known as "Jack," jokingly referred to *Surprised by Joy*, his bestselling autobiography, as "Suppressed by Jack."
8. Marcus, *Listening*, 172.
9. See Kathleen Long Bostrom, *Winning Authors: Profiles of the Newbery Medalists* (Westport, CT: Libraries Unlimited, 2003), 137.
10. L'Engle, *Quiet*, 197.
11. Marcus, *Listening*, 179–80.

12. Cynthia Zarin, "The Storyteller: Fact, Fiction, and the Books of Madeleine L'Engle," *The New Yorker*, April 12, 2004, accessed May 5, 2018. https://www.newyorker.com/magazine/ 2004/04/12/the-storyteller-cynthia-zarin.

13. L'Engle, *Quiet*, 93.

14. L'Engle, *Quiet*, 93.

15. Madeleine L'Engle, *Meet the Austins* (New York: Square Fish / Macmillan / Farrar, Straus & Giroux, 1960), 15.

16. See L'Engle, *Walking*, 223–24.

17. Marcus, *Listening*, 204.

18. Marcus, *Listening*, 297.

19. Cara Parks, "Ironing Out the Wrinkles—The Complexities of Madeleine L'Engle," *The New Republic*, Nov. 27, 2012, accessed May 5, 2018. https://newrepublic.com/article/110453/ wrinkle-in-time-complexities-madeline-lengle-leonard-marcus.

20. L'Engle, *Walking*, 164.

21. L'Engle, *Walking*, 47.

22. L'Engle, *Princess*, viii–ix.

23. L'Engle, *Princess*, x.

24. Marcus, *Listening*, 158.

25. Calvin Miller, "The Blue Tattoo" in *Christhaven*, 68.

26. Madeleine L'Engle, afterword to *Beyond Belief: What the Martyrs Said to God* by Duane W. H. Arnold and Robert Hudson (Grand Rapids, MI: Zondervan, 2002), 135.

Chapter 7: Light in the Darkness

1. L'Engle, *Rock*, 11.

2. From chapter 27 of *The Revelations of Divine Love* by St Julian of Norwich: "But Jesus, who in this Vision informed me of all that is needful to me, answered by this word and said: *It behoved that there should be sin; but all shall be well, and all shall be well, and all manner of thing shall be well.*"

3. In yet another example from one of her Wheaton College lectures, she said, "I don't know what happens often, but I know that ultimately, as Lady Julian of Norwich said, 'All shall

be well. All is in God's hand, and God is ultimately in control of creation.' We have free will, that tiny pearl; but God is in control of creation." Chase, *Herself*, 272.

4. L'Engle, *Walking*, 185–86.

5. Voiklis and Roy, *Becoming Madeleine*, 67.

6. L'Engle, *Two-Part Invention*, 61.

7. Maria Rooney, *Mothers and Daughters*, with Madeleine L'Engle, 7.

8. L'Engle, *Great-Grandmother*, part 1, chapter 3, Kindle edition.

9. Madeleine L'Engle, from the Q&A following her plenary "The Cosmic Questions" at the 1996 Calvin College Festival of Faith and Writing, accessed via the festival archives on May 5, 2018. https://soundcloud.com/user-309235021/ref-a03218-engle -evening-event/s-Zyu4u.

10. L'Engle, *Rock*, 266.

11. Hettinga, *Presenting*, 14.

12. L'Engle, *Door*, 46.

13. L'Engle, *Walking*, 165–66.

14. L'Engle, *Wrinkle*, 89.

15. L'Engle, *Irrational Season*, 28.

16. For example, Van Kuiken writes in "The Gospel of Madeleine L'Engle," "Despite their differences, L'Engle pictures the good and evil characters in *Many Waters* as being brothers, leaving the distinct impression that God and Satan will, at some point in time, be united again."

17. Scientific theory once held that Mercury didn't rotate like other planets, and thus had a permanent dark side that never saw the sun. This theory has since been challenged.

18. Michael O'Brien, *A Landscape with Dragons: The Battle for Your Child's Mind* (San Francisco: Ignatius Press, 1998), 103.

19. See St. Irenaeus's second-century treatise *Against Heresies*, particularly book 3.

20. L'Engle, "Do I Dare Disturb the Universe?" Kindle edition.

21. L'Engle, during an on-stage conversation with Luci Shaw at the 1996 Calvin College Festival of Faith and Writing, accessed via

the festival archives on May 5, 2018. https://soundcloud.com/
user-309235021/ref-a03220-shaw-and-lengle-1996/s-kRhJO.

22. L'Engle, *Quiet.* Kindle edition.

23. L'Engle, *Good*, 37.

24. Madeleine L'Engle, interviewed by Bob Abernethy in a PBS episode
of *Religion & Ethics NewsWeekly*, Nov. 17, 2000, accessed May
5, 2018. http://www.pbs.org/wnet/religionandethics/2012/02/10/
november-17-2000-madeleine-lengle/3639/.

25. Mother Teresa, *Come Be My Light: The Private Writings of
the "Saint of Calcutta"* ed. Brian Kolodiejchuk (New York:
Doubleday, a division of Random House, Inc., 2007), 163.

26. Mother Teresa, *Come Be My Light*, 214.

27. L'Engle, *Walking*, 189.

28. L'Engle, *Walking*, 202–3.

29. Madeleine L'Engle, Odyssey Networks interview posted
posthumously, July 30, 2010, accessed May 5, 2018. https://
www.youtube.com/watch?v=yCVf_Fooqhk.

30. L'Engle, *Good*, 133.

31. L'Engle, *Great-Grandmother*, part 1, chapter 12, Kindle edition.

32. L'Engle, *Two-Part Invention*, part 2, chapter 9, Kindle edition.

33. Marcus, *Listening*, 98.

34. L'Engle, *Walking*, 119.

35. Luci Shaw, first printed in *Harvesting Fog* (Pinyon Publishing,
2010). Used by permission of Pinyon Publishing, 23847 V66
Trail, Montrose, Colorado 81403.

36. Annie Dillard, *The Writing Life* in *Three by Annie Dillard*
(New York: Perennial / HarperCollins, 1990), 568.

Epilogue: Tesser Well

1. L'Engle, *Wrinkle*, 172.

2. L'Engle, *Wrinkle*, 172.

3. L'Engle, *Irrational Season*, 118.

4. L'Engle, *Irrational Season*, 118.

5. Enger, *Penguins*, xiii.

6. L'Engle, Calvin festival plenary Q&A.

RECOMMENDED BOOKS

By Madeleine L'Engle

Walking on Water: Reflections on Faith and Art
The Rock That Is Higher: Story as Truth
A Circle of Quiet
A Wrinkle in Time
A Wind in the Door
A Swiftly Tilting Planet
Meet the Austins
A Ring of Endless Light
A Live Coal in the Sea
*The Ordering of Love: The New and Collected Poems of
    Madeleine L'Engle*
Madeleine L'Engle Herself compiled by Carole F. Chase

About Madeleine L'Engle

*Becoming Madeleine: A Biography of the Author of A Wrinkle
    in Time by Her Granddaughters* by Charlotte Jones Voiklis
    and Léna Roy
Presenting Madeleine L'Engle by Donald R. Hettinga
*Listening for Madeleine: A Portrait of Madeleine L'Engle in
    Many Voices* by Leonard Marcus